MY LIFE STAMP

● ●

As a youth with little a plan,
My dad oft asked,
"What footprints are you going to leave in the sand?"

It meant little then,
But with time,
This became a motivating line.

If up to me,
What will be,
My ultimate legacy?

A legacy for me,
It would seem,
A far off, lofty dream.

After all, who am I?
I'm just average,
Somewhat shy.

Then I realized something you see,
It is up to me,
My ultimate legacy.

Social media, search,
Mobile, and more,
Leave digital footprints on the floor.

Digital shadows,
If you will,
Following all that I fulfill.

My grandchildren and great grandchildren,
What will they see and think of me?
What is my digital legacy?

● ● ● ● ●

Will they see that I pursued my dream,
Or that I settled,
For something in-between?

That I lived a life doing things I loved,
Or one filled with,
Should of, could of?

Digital footprints remain for all time,
So I can't commit,
The ultimate crime.

What is that crime, you say?
It is, of course,
Not seizing the day.

Yes, before I die,
I'd rather fail,
Than not even try,

I will reach for the sky,
Laugh,
And cry.

I'll cry from joy not sorrow,
Because I lived for today
And planned for tomorrow.

My legacy,
You see,
Is truly up to me.

That's my view,
But, now I ask,
What will you do?

Written by Erik Qualman from his book *Digital Leader*

* * * *

ERIK QUALMAN

EQUALMAN STUDIOS
Cambridge MA

For my beautiful wife and daughters.

You make the world a better place.

● ● ● ● ●

• • • • •

"We don't have a choice on whether we do social & mobile, the choice is in how well we do it."

• • • • •

The above quote seems illogical. After all, do I not have a choice regarding my use of social and mobile outlets or any new technology? Would avoidance of these new tools protect my reputation?

You could choose the path of technology avoidance, but it would be increasingly difficult to succeed without these digital tools and your reputation could still be compromised. Regardless if you elect to use social media or have a digital presence, people will be looking for you online. When you do not create and manage your digital reputation, you allow others to do this for you. Would you rather have influence over your reputation, or give that control to others?

For example, research indicates that 92% of children under the age of two already have a digital posting about them.[1] Yes, what happens offline stays online. This is a fundamental shift in society. It is a shift that many of us, from students to teachers to CEOs, have failed to grasp. By reading this book, you have made the choice to produce and protect your best reputation. Nice choice.

TABLE OF CONTENTS

INTRODUCTION

As a young person, you are experiencing great time of exploration. It is a time where you can figure out who you are and who you want to be. One of the greatest strengths of the Internet is its ability to allow people to engage, connect, play and learn more about themselves. Perhaps you're a LGBT student who has not had the possibility to meet others to share insights, opportunities and challenges. Or perhaps you want to reinvent yourself and find new interests. Or maybe you want to join a fraternity or sorority in college and develop deep relationships with new people. Be genuine in your online interactions and you will be surprised with the amazing opportunities you will be presented. It is a great way for you to learn to be comfortable in your own skin. Who do you want to be?

During this time of youthful exploration, sometimes we make choices we later regret. Maybe we chose an unfortunate hairstyle or maybe we make a mistake in one of our relationships. Unlike generations before you, however, your exploration, your evolution and your missteps are much more likely to be public. They are also more likely to follow you after college. This shouldn't scare you, but it should make you think about what you post and be aware of what others post about you. Remember what sometimes seems like a good idea at the time can, in retrospect, be a poor decision.

This book is filled with great examples of young people just like you that have used the digital tools at their fingertips to be able to drive change, start a company or share their ideas and thoughts with the world. You'll read about how students from Western Illinois University started an #unselfie campaign to share acts of kindness and capture stories of social good on campus. In our success stories section, you can read about how one young woman from Michigan State University started a blog called *52 Cups* documenting a year filled with 52 different meetings she had over coffee with thought leaders, authors and university presidents. Finally, you'll read about a variety of different students that are using social media to produce a strong digital identity that will help them achieve their biggest aspirations and career goals. While there are some drawbacks to growing up in the digital age, we think that after reading this book, you'll find that the benefits far outweigh these disadvantages.

This book can be read in a day, but referenced for a lifetime. Everyone important to you deserves this gift. Its 36 essential rules ensure you produce and **preserve your most important asset — your reputation.**

One of the best ways to learn is by understanding the stories of those that came before you. This book includes many real world examples of students and individuals doing awesome and extraordinary things. We also highlight stories of individuals who have made mistakes online. These stories are referenced and publicly available online, but in some cases we have chosen to only include the individuals' first names. The reason for this is that, where we can, we do not wish to contribute to spreading an unfortunate story that may, in some cases, follow these people the rest of their lives. One of the tenets of this book is to be kind to others.

THE NEW RULES OF REPUTATION

1. Common sense is not that common
2. Live as though your mother is watching
3. KISS: Keep It Super Simple
4. 100% LinkedIn profile completion
5. Don't post whispers
6. Integrity & reputation are now one
7. What's your digital compass?
8. Be "FLAWsome"
9. Privacy is your problem
10. Have one digital identity
11. Complain = Digital Pain
12. Post it forward
13. Network before you need your network
14. Praise publicly, criticize privately
15. Words: Measure twice, post once
16. The three-second rule
17. We will make digital mistakes—how we handle them defines us

18. Multitasking = Mistakes

19. A picture is worth a thousand words

20. It's not the crime, but the cover-up

21. Make ginormous public goals

22. Face-2-Face cannot be replaced

23. Tinderbox Topics—Caution!

24. The power of a letter

25. Cyberbullying: Don't enable it

26. Be a digital change agent

27. Be genuine

28. Fail fast, fail forward, fail better

29. Freedom of choice — Not freedom from consequence

30. Join your campus community online

31. You represent your school, organization, team & family

32. Be a Baker not an Eater

33. Your Legacy = Digital Footprints + Digital Shadows

34. Surround yourself with success

35. Watch your language

36. Teach & train your fellow students, friends and family

• • • • •

"A man is the sum of his actions,
of what he has done,
of what he can do, nothing else."

GANDHI

• • • • •

$$\equiv \left(\begin{array}{c} \mathcal{N}o. \\ 1 \end{array}\right) \equiv$$

Common Sense is Not That Common

- Smart people make costly gaffes by posting items digitally without using common sense. They also commit inappropriate acts offline and pay the price when these indiscretions are discovered online. In today's world, your offline and online actions will always be discovered!

- The new reputation rules in this book will help you increase your digital common sense and avoid public digital blunders. These easy to remember concepts will not only help you survive, but also thrive in this digital age. You will present and protect your best self.

- Already have digital common sense? Gift this book to a person you care about who is not so savvy (e.g., co-worker, employee, teammate, spouse, son). For a refresher, I encourage you to review these rules occasionally as well.

- When it comes to your digital reputation, it is always best to have command of your destiny. In today's world, your digital reputation is your reputation.

- 1 in 3 people regret something they posted online.[2] Perhaps you have some regrets. Swearing or using hateful language in a post? An emotionally charged outburst? An unflattering photo of you drinking or doing something inappropriate? A meme or joke that's in poor taste? Something that reflects poorly on your school, a student organization you're involved in, or your athletic team? These things happen to just about everyone.

- The good news is that you have this book to be able to help you navigate these situations and be able to fail fast and forward. Keep reading for tips on how to handle these regretful posts, and learn how to take the steps to avoid them in the future.

ACTION ITEM

Google your name; search results often indicate how the world sees you. Make sure to click also on the "images" and "videos" tabs to see any particular media that has been posted of you.

If you find disconcerting content about yourself, you can submit a request to Google for its removal here:

www.google.com/webmasters/tools/removals

• • • • •

"The people who are worried about privacy have a legitimate worry. But, we live in a complex world where you're going to have to need a level of security greater than you did back in the olden days, if you will. And, our laws and our interpretation of the Constitution, I think, have to change."

MICHAEL BLOOMBERG

• • • • •

No. 2

Live as Though Your Family is Watching

- While family may look differently for everyone, we typically use this word to describe those closest to us and those that hold us to our highest standards. Whether this is your blood relatives like a mother and father, or maybe your closest friends, or even your teammates, we all have people that believe in us and care about us. We should live as though these individuals are able to see all that we do online; because the truth is that they can see it. Many stories in this book illustrate how the perceived boundaries on the Internet are often broken in this transparent world.

- Rule of thumb: If it's something that would embarrass the person you hold dearest, do not do it offline and do not post it online. Fifty-one percent of employers in the United States report that they have rejected candidates because of information posted in social media.[3]

- Always think twice before you press the send button.

- Advances in wearable technology combined with decreasing costs of video storage indicate that soon, everything will be recorded.

- Your judgment can be impaired when you've been drinking alcohol. Even if you do not post your party pictures from spring break or a house party, someone else will.

ACTION ITEM

Although you should never completely rely on your privacy settings keeping items private, they can act as a safeguard. Log in to your favorite social and mobile tools/apps and check your settings. Some social networks, such as Facebook have a "View as" feature so you can check to see how others see you and what they see. Or use the Google Chrome Incognito setting to view your profiles – this also shows you what others see.

• • • • •

"It takes 20 years to build a reputation and five minutes to ruin it. If you think about that, you'll do things differently."

WARREN BUFFETT

• • • • •

LEARNING MOMENT

There were dangerous riots and looting of stores in Vancouver, Canada, following the Vancouver Canucks loss in Game 7 of the Stanley Cup hockey finals. Many looters initially escaped police punishment, but were arrested several days later.

How were they caught? Civilians helped police find wrong doers via photos that were posted on Facebook and Twitter. From these photos, "Digital Deputies" and "Digital Vigilantes" identified individuals who had committed criminal activity.

LESSON: The good outnumber the bad, always have and always will and now they have smartphones with cameras.

LEARNING MOMENT

Alanah Pearce is a Queensland video game reviewer with a very popular YouTube channel. When the 21-year-old journalist had enough with the hateful comments from young male fans threatening to sexually assault her, she took a unique and powerful approach to responding to the online harassment. Pearce looked into the most sexually aggressive messages a little further and noticed that it was not coming from adult men but from young.

She decided that a rational response to their comments would not work, so she took a more creative approach. She did some research and found their mothers online. She then shared the sexually aggressive comments with their mothers. See a tweet from Pearce about one of the interactions with a harasser's mother that went viral.[4]

LESSON: If you are doing something online that you're mother would be ashamed of then you probably shouldn't be doing it. Anyone with a smartphone can track down a parent, family member or even your boss to share what you are posting.

KISS: Keep It Super Simple

- Steve Jobs was proud of the things he and Apple decided *NOT* to do. If you try to stand for everything, then you stand for nothing. Facebook founder Mark Zuckerberg discovered that "...the trick isn't adding stuff, it's taking away."[5]

- Determine what you want to stand for as an individual. You need to know *who* you want to be before you determine *what* you want to achieve. For example the small business or a non-profit you start is the "what," but you are the "who" that people will remember long after that entity is gone.

- Your online identity will evolve as you do. This is natural. People appreciate someone being genuine about their growth.

- Many of us complicate our lives by trying to be everything to everyone. This makes our reputation difficult to manage. Life in the digital age is complex; those who simplify it win.

- You don't need a triple or quadruple major. You don't need to be the president of every single club on campus. Instead of aiming for broad and shallow, focus on a few things with depth. Find your niche.

ACTION ITEM

On a regular basis, reevaluate your involvement on campus and online. Are there distractions in your life? Areas where you can dig deeper? Step back and make some conscious choices.

ACTION ITEM

For your digital presence, try to be consistent across all social networks by using the same photograph – this also keeps it simple. Need a good photograph? Grab a friend that is good at photography and pick a location with proper lighting (lighting should be in front of you). As famous author and Internet Guru Guy Kawasaki suggests (*The Art of Social Media*) the purpose of your profile photo should give the impression that you are likeable, trustworthy and competent. Here are 4 tips from a personal interview I conducted with Kawasaki that will help put your best face forward:

4 Tips For Getting The Best Profile Picture

Getting a good profile picture is important for two reasons. First, it validates who you are, as there may be more than one person with you're name. Second, it supports the narrative that you are likeable, competent, and trustworthy. Here are a few tips to help you get the best picture for your profiles.

- **Focus on your face:** There's no room for your family, dogs or a school mascot.

- **Go asymmetrical:** Symmetry makes a photo less interesting. Don't put your face in the middle. Use hypothetical vertical lines to divide your photo into thirds and place your eyes on one of these lines (see image below)

continued...

ACTION ITEM (continued)

- **Face the light:** The source of light should come from in front of you.
- **Think big:** Upload a photo that is at least 600 pixels wide. While people will most often be scanning your posts and see the postage side image, when they click on one of your posts they will see a crisp, clear and large photo of you. It's important to have this 600-pixels-wide image.

• • • • •

"If you have more than three priorities, then you don't have any."

JIM COLLINS, AUTHOR OF *GOOD TO GREAT*

• • • • •

LEARNING MOMENT

A University of London study revealed that reading digital messages while performing another cognitive task decreased the IQ in some male participants by 15 points putting some in the range of an 8-year-old child. This decrease is equivalent to not sleeping at night.[6]

LESSON: Eliminating multitasking puts you on a path to simplification & success.

100% LinkedIn Profile

- LinkedIn is rapidly replacing the paper resume. 93% of companies use LinkedIn to research candidates.[7] Recruiters are often reviewing social profiles to identify mutual connections and evaluate writing samples or design work.

- 42% of the time recruiters find items online that cause them to dismiss a candidate.[8]

- LinkedIn provides networks where you can engage with alumni. 80% of jobs are obtained through relationships and connections.[9]

- LinkedIn allows you to see profiles of your college or university, including what industries alumni work in, what companies they work for, and the top skills they attain. Use this information when researching careers and potential jobs.

- According to the US Department of Labor, 65% of today's grade school children will end up in jobs that haven't even been invented yet.[10] Staying continually fresh and renewed professionally is important.

- Research from LinkedIn indicates that if your LinkedIn profile is 100% complete, you will receive **40x more job and business opportunities** than someone who doesn't have a complete profile.[11]

- LinkedIn profiles show up high in Google search results. This is particularly helpful for those who do not have a substantial digital presence (i.e., a blog, company website, YouTube channel).

- LinkedIn indicates in the upper right hand corner of your profile how strong and complete your profile is. If it's incomplete, LinkedIn will indicate if you forgot to post a profile photo, recommendations or previous jobs. Many career services & development offices within schools and universities are now assisting students with their LinkedIn presence.

ACTION ITEM

If you don't have a LinkedIn profile, create one. If you have a LinkedIn profile, update it.

Join groups and communities on LinkedIn that align with your major and career interests. Read what others are saying. Consider posting your own comments.

• • • • •

"A brand for a company is like a reputation for a person. You earn a good reputation by trying to do hard things well."

JEFF BEZOS

• • • • •

LEARNING MOMENTS

David T. Stevens signed up for LinkedIn, hoping it would help him network for his sales job with KEZR and KBAY radio in San Jose, California. Several months later, the economy took a turn for the worse, and Stevens found himself looking for work. As he headed out on his last day, he decided to post on LinkedIn, "Up for Grabs. Who wants me?"

On his ride home, he received a call from one of his contacts on LinkedIn who knew of an open job. Another LinkedIn connection recommended him to the hiring manager for this position. Stevens scheduled an interview and two weeks later, he was working for his new organization. "I was like, this is awesome," recalls Stevens, 31. "That was a miracle, but I had my doubts it could happen."[12]

LESSON: Digital tools expedite the process for many things that used to take multiple steps and several weeks. This is a great example of how quickly one can use LinkedIn to obtain their next job, interview, or important meeting.

• • • • •

Using the LinkedIn platform, an applicant can apply to multiple jobs with just one click. Using this functionality on LinkedIn, the Samuel Curtis Johnson Graduate School of Management at Cornell University has streamlined their admissions process to allow candidates to apply through LinkedIn. Cornell announced this new process on July 8, 2014 for certain MBA programs. Applicants can use their LinkedIn profile to fill in key components of the application. This new system is a win-win, as it will make the process more efficient for applicants and lessens the duplication of efforts for admissions officers that are already researching candidates on LinkedIn.[13]

continued...

LEARNING MOMENTS
(continued)

LESSON: When one of the country's top MBA programs uses LinkedIn as part of their application process, it sends a very important message to students about being active on this network. All signs point to LinkedIn as replacing the paper resume and this is just one more example of how it is happening. Some schools and universities are requiring their students to join LinkedIn as part of the enrollment process.

• • • • •

"When one door of happiness closes, another opens, but often we look so long at the closed door that we do not see the one that has been opened for us."

HELEN KELLER

• • • • •

No. 5

Don't Post Whispers

- If you'd whisper it offline, do not post it online.

- With the rise in anonymous social platforms like Facebook rooms, Yik Yak and Unseen, many people are posting things online they would never say in public. Don't be fooled, if you post something on one of these anonymous sites where you threaten to hurt others, those sites must turn over your IP address to the authorities. Before you post something anonymously, decide whether you would be comfortable saying this in public.

- If pondering whether something is appropriate to post online, ask yourself: *Would I tell this to a large group of people in-person?* If the answer is "no" or "maybe not," do not post it.

- Most whispered conversations do not reflect your best self.

- Your friends and followers will discover if you are posting whispers. You will quickly develop a reputation as someone who posts private information.

- If someone were to hear your offline whispers, they could always post it digitally.

- Do not be a bystander when it comes to whispers. Learn how to confront someone, with care and tact, when they post something you think is inappropriate. In many cases, this may be best done in person, offline.

LEARNING MOMENTS

A star football running back revealed an MRI of his hamstring injury on Twitter. This is a big "no-no," since your competitors are also on Twitter and will use this injury information to their advantage in the football game.

If you work at a business and aren't sure if something is secret or proprietary, do not post it until you are 100% sure it's OK. Do not give your competitors digital ammunition that can be later used against you.

If you hear a secret about someone or some juicy gossip, make sure it stops with you. The worst thing you can do for others and your own reputation is to post this information digitally. This will ultimately reflect poorly on you.

LESSON: Nefarious activity or secrets should be revealed; all other secrets are generally best kept secrets.

• • • • •

Many students hold a false reality about the anonymous nature of Yik Yak, Snapchat and other similar tools. In numerous cases students are being arrested and charged with crimes for posting threatening comments on these social media outlets. Ranging from misdemeanors to felonies, these criminal charges for digital threats can include:

• Terroristic threatening;
• Unlawful use of a digital device;
• Using a digital device to threaten to cause injury;
• Stalking or harassment; or
• Disorderly conduct.[14]

Once campus police are notified of a seemingly anonymous threat, campus police or local law enforcement can secure a subpoena requiring Yik Yak or other such tools to share the user's IP address and even the GPS location where the post originated. With this information, law enforcement and University administrators can easily identify who posted the threats.

continued...

LEARNING MOMENTS (continued)

An example of this type of arrest happened to former Towson State University student Matthew. After posting a threat to the Towson campus, Matthew was banned from campus, arrested, and charged with a series of criminal offenses within 24 hours. During the Fall 2014 semester, there were at least a dozen similar incidents on campuses across the country including the University of North Carolina[15], State University of New York (SUNY) at Albany[16], and The University of Southern Mississippi[17] among several more institutions.

LESSON: Anonymous is never anonymous. Law enforcement and university leaders take campus safety seriously, and have the cooperation of Yik Yak in identifying anyone who threatens to act violently.

· · · · ·

"We don't get a chance to do that many things, and everyone should be really excellent. Because this is our life ... life is brief, and then you die, you know?"

STEVE JOBS

· · · · ·

Integrity & Reputation are Now One

- Integrity is what you do behind closed doors or when you think nobody is watching. Integrity is the true essence of who you are, your beliefs and your values.

- Reputation is the public perception of who you are. It's how others view your integrity or strong moral principles.

- As a result of digital tools and connectivity, the difference between your integrity and reputation is now zero. Everything we do or say is broadcast to the world. The result? **Reputation = Integrity.**

ACTION ITEM

Ask a trusted friend, advisor, or someone who has known you for a long time how they would describe your values and reputation. Pay attention to their answer. Do you like what they have to say or do you want to make changes in your life?

LEARNING MOMENT

Meghan Vogel, a junior at Ohio's West Liberty-Salem High School, won the state's 1,600-meter race, but she became an even greater champion by finishing last in another race. Why does her last place finish have millions of views on YouTube?

In the 3,200-meter race, Vogel was 50 meters from the finish line when another runner, Arden McMath of Arlington High School, collapsed. Rather than run past her, Vogel stopped on the track and carried her fallen competitor across the finish line, making certain that McMath finished ahead of her in the race.

"Helping her across the finish line was a lot more satisfying than winning the state championship," Vogel told the News-Sun.

"I've never seen that," said Arlington coach Paul Hunter. "What a selfless act. That's real sportsmanship."[18]

VIDEO: http://bit.ly/1L3bDL7

LESSON: Finishing first has many different definitions. Run your race.

• • • • •

"The way to gain a good reputation is to endeavor to be what you desire to appear."

SOCRATES

• • • • • •

LEARNING MOMENT

On Gay Pride Day, Oreo posted an image of their iconic chocolate wafer cookie on social media. This made news because the traditional white cream filling was replaced with the colors of the rainbow and the word "Pride" beneath it. This support of the gay community was controversial, but it was authentic in what Oreo believes in. The campaign won numerous awards and the positives outweighed the negatives. Specifically, Oreo doubled their daily fans from 25,000 per day to 50,000 per day, helping their approach. They also had 80,000 people share the post, which equated to a 4929% increase over normal sharing activity for Oreo.[19]

JUNE 25 | PRIDE

LESSON: When a brand is true to its values, they will often be rewarded with the love of their followers and fans.

What's Your Digital Compass?

- Write a digital compass. Keep it simple—140 characters or less. What do you want people to find when they search Google? Set your sights high. For example, mine is:

  Be a "Digital Dale Carnegie" by inspiring others to achieve their best life, leadership and legacy while honoring God and Family.

- Think of this as a moral compass, the guiding light for your ultimate legacy. Whenever you are faced with a difficult decision or situation, use this as your guide.

- It's helpful to write down what you want the most important people in your life to say about you at your funeral. From this exercise, you will notice you aren't writing down accomplishments (fastest, smartest, best), but more profound concepts—how did your presence uplift others? We no longer have to wait for our funeral to hear what people are saying about us. We know what people are posting about us.

- Social media can be a powerful tool to use in organizing for activism, social change and civic engagement. What are the causes that matter to you? How can you bring this passion online?

- For some, their online tools enable their digital compass, for others, online engagement is a part of their digital compass. Is a digital life integral to what you want to achieve in life?

- If you are a military veteran going to college for the first time, this is a great opportunity to establish who you are and what you want your next phase in life to be. Take advantage of it.

ACTION ITEM

Post your personal digital compass online with the hashtag #digitalcompass and read the contributions of others.

LEARNING MOMENT

At the young age of three, Dyrk Burcie was diagnosed with pediatric liver cancer. Dyrk's father was a firefighter and Dyrk certainly had the fighting spirit. This spirit soon became known as "Dyrk Strong." As Dyrk battled this terminal disease, local fire stations started posting images of "Dyrk" and "Dyrk Strong."

The fire stations looked for unique ways to send their support for this courageous boy. Fire stations became creative by spelling the name "Dyrk" letter-by-letter in fire or casting it alongside the tallest ladder on the fire truck.

Soon, the cause spread globally, with thousands of people posting images dedicated to Dyrk and his cancer prevention cause. Dyrk's courage showcases that in today's digital era, mountains can be moved and hearts can be connected as the communication barriers of time and distance are removed.

Dyrk died in peace after his fourth birthday, but his digital legacy lives on forever.

More on Dyrk: http://bit.ly/dyrk-strong

LESSON: Take inspiration from our hero Dyrk by leaving a legacy that matters.

Be FLAWsome

- The world is a better place because of everyone's imperfections.

- Admit and own your flaws either as an organization, institution, department or as an individual and the world will think you are awesome.

- Being "FLAWsome" [20] is admitting that you aren't perfect. You are awesome because of your flaws. FLAWsome is described as owning your mistakes and taking the necessary steps to correct them. It's about turning a negative into a positive (such as making digital lemonade out of digital lemons).

- When living in close quarters with others, such as in a residence hall or fraternity or sorority house, it is easy to think that behaviors and actions are the norm when in reality they are not. Chart your own path. Avoid the mistakes of others.

- Making a mistake as a student organization or as an individual is your opportunity to show everyone that you are awesome by caring enough to correct the flaw. 83% of people liked or loved that an organization responded to a complaint on Twitter. Yet, 76% of people who complain on Twitter do not receive a response from an organization. [21]

LEARNING MOMENT

A young woman at the Red Cross thought she was posting to her own Twitter account, but accidentally hit the button for the Red Cross Twitter account. She posted *"Ryan found two more 4 packs of Dogfish Head's Midas Touch beer, when we drink we do it right."* A young man at the Red Cross saw this mistake and immediately posted on Twitter *"We've deleted the rogue tweet, but rest assured the Red Cross is sober and we've confiscated the keys."*

The result? The beer company suggested that instead of drinking a pint of beer, beer drinkers should consider donating a pint of blood to the Red Cross. Donations for the Red Cross increased dramatically that week. By using humor, the Red Cross showed they are simply people trying to help people. They turned a potential negative situation into a positive one. They were FLAWsome!

I too witnessed this first hand. Some of my most ardent literary critics often become my biggest supporters when I listen to what they say and admit that I made a grammatical error or acknowledge that a chapter in the book isn't "up to snuff."

FedEx also discovered that a customer is three times more likely to remain a steady customer when resolving a customer's complaint, as compared to a person who never experienced a problem with FedEx.

continued...

LEARNING MOMENT (continued)

LESSON: Rather than attempting to present a perfect digital profile, proudly present yourself—*"here I am, warts and all!"* Also, speed wins. A quick, short response in four minutes is better than the perfect response four days later.

More on FLAWsome here:
www.trendwatching.com/trends/FLAWsome/

*Hat tip: Ann Handley first introduced me to this concept

• • • • •

"I have as much privacy as a goldfish in a bowl."

PRINCESS MARGARET

• • • • • •

Privacy is Your Problem

- Do not assume that someone else is looking out for your digital privacy.

- Be mindful about posting an image that might have your personal information on it. For instance, posting an image of your acceptance letter to your first choice school might seem like a great idea at the time but be careful not to share your home address, school ID #, and any other personal information in the process.

- One in four victims of stalking report that the stalker used technology, such as computers, GPS devices or hidden cameras, to track the victim's daily activities.[22]

- Be very careful when using GPS tracking apps like MapMyRun, Nike+ running and Foursquare. Sharing your progress towards a fitness goal can be very rewarding, but if you share your running path of choice with the world, you could be giving that information to the wrong people. Someone could easily figure out where and when you will be taking your next run, or use Foursquare to find out the exact location where you are grabbing coffee and studying. Cyberstalking can easily cross the threshold into the offline world and become a serious threat to your safety. Be mindful of the information you share on social media about your whereabouts.

- Nearly 75 percent of college stalking victims forgo contacting law enforcement.[23] *This is not good.* If you believe you are being stalked, report it immediately. Unfortunately, many times stalking can start out as something that feels harmless and can escalate quickly.

- Facebook, Twitter and even the FBI (see below), despite their best intentions and privacy tools, do not care nearly as much about your privacy as you should.

- You need to take ownership of your privacy and identity. Stay abreast of security breaches involving companies you use.

- Pay attention to emails discussing security breaches, but never click on these emails, as they could be phishing scams. Instead, visit the company site directly by typing in the Web address. This will save you from accidentally clicking on a phishing scam, including fake emails or websites attempting to obtain your personal information.

- Periodically review free credit rating reports from the appropriate agencies in your country. These credit reports often can alert you to a potential digital security breach involving your personal data. A good credit score is important for one to obtain good rates on car loans, mortgages, some student loans, etc.

LEARNING MOMENT

The Antisec hacker group reported stealing 12 million Apple IDs from the computer of an FBI agent. This hacker group then posted the personal information of some of these IDs online. Once someone has your ID they can often use it to buy items with your credit card or bank account.[24]

LESSON: If the FBI can be hacked, so can you.

• • • • •

"Once you've lost your privacy,
you realize you've lost
an extremely valuable thing."

BILLY GRAHAM

• • • • •

ACTION ITEM

Review the passwords you have set for your accounts. If there are any passwords that someone could easily guess (i.e., password, 12345, your last name), take a moment to change them. Passwords that are longer are harder to guess. Perhaps pick a phrase that will motivate you every time you enter it, and make that your password. If you can add numbers, capitals and alphanumeric symbols (like $ or !), these will strengthen your password. You should often make a habit of frequently changing your passwords.

• • • • •

"Privacy is one of the biggest problems
in this new electronic age."

ANDY GROVE

• • • • •

= (No. 10) =

Have One Digital Identity

- As a student, you need to start thinking deliberately about your digital identity. You will be more successful in any career path you choose if your presence across all social and mobile platforms is consistent.

- With rare exceptions, it is best to have only one account/profile for each digital network, including avoiding having four different Facebook profiles. Having only one account is also easier to maintain—and less stressful (see rule #3 Simplify)!

- Many people have discovered that having a LinkedIn account for their business contacts and a Facebook account for their personal contacts is a great approach. If you aren't comfortable when your boss wants to connect with you on Facebook, kindly ask him/her to connect with you on LinkedIn and encourage your boss to write you a LinkedIn recommendation! Keep in mind, like it or not, the days of having a work personality and a completely different weekend personality are over.

- Be yourself! It is much easier than pretending to be someone else. The rules in this book are guidelines; they aren't designed to make you a robot. Let your own unique personality shine online.

ACTION ITEM

There are advantages to having a consistent username across email and social media platforms. Consider "squatting" your name on other services, even if you don't intend to use them frequently, so you can ensure that others don't take your name.

LEARNING MOMENTS

The FBI uncovered U.S. Central Intelligence Director General David Petraeus's trail of deceit and extramarital affair. Petraeus and U.S. Army Lieutenant, Paula Broadwell, were having an affair. Despite Petraeus's expansive knowledge of digital espionage, the FBI was eventually able to find some digital breadcrumbs indicting the two. Petraeus and Broadwell had set up a communication system using fake names via free webmail accounts and exchanged messages without encryption tools. They would share an email account with one saving a message in the draft's folder and the other deleting the message after it was read.

This was one of the biggest scandals in history and Petraeus was forced to tender his resignation as Director of the CIA to President Barack Obama.[25]

LESSON: If the Director of the CIA can't cover his tracks, do not think you will succeed in leading a double life.

• • • • •

"You have one identity. The days of you having a different image for your work friends or co-workers and for the other people you know are probably coming to an end pretty quickly… Having two identities for yourself is an example of a lack of integrity."[26]

— Mark Zuckerberg, Facebook Founder & CEO

LESSON: Become one personal brand both offline and online.

Complain=Digital Pain

- Complaining is negative energy and the enemy of greatness.

- Remember: Anything you post online is in "ink," not "pencil." Do you want your digital footprint littered with complaints starting while you are in school?

- If you experience poor customer service and want to express it online, do it constructively. Many companies, organizations and offices will work with you to address your concerns.

- What you post reflects not just on you, but also on the student organizations, teams and clubs to which you belong. Think about how this will reflect on your groups.

- It's imperative not to complain about a particular person. Think how you feel when you see a post that says, "<your name> is a jerk!"

- The average person complains between 15-30 times per day. Your digital footprint, or what you post online, will positively stand out from other students simply by not complaining.[27]

LEARNING MOMENTS

A young man was working for an online agency and Chrysler was their marquee client. Part of his job was to assist Chrysler with its Twitter account. On one particular day, he had a very difficult commute to work.

To help relieve his frustration, he posted to his Twitter account, *"I find it ironic that Detroit is known as the #motorcity and yet no one here knows how to fu***** drive."* Unfortunately, he hit the wrong button and instead of posting to his private Twitter account, he posted this on the Chrysler Twitter account for millions to see. He and his agency where quickly fired. Complaining often negatively impacts the complainer, so rise above it.[28]

Remember average person complains roughly 23 times per day.[29] Be above average—stop complaining.

A good way to practice not complaining is to track your progress. For each complaint-free day, put a rubber band on your wrist. Try to accumulate seven days in a row without a complaint. Good luck!

LESSON: Be wary of texting and tweeting in the heat of the moment.

• • • • •

Avoid perpetuating "digital hate" and online rage.[30] One example of this is students of the University of Illinois backlashing against Chancellor Phyllis Wise for not declaring a "snow day." The backlash included cyberbullying of Wise on Twitter with a hashtag of choice. One example of a tweet was, "In room with Phyllis Wise, Adolf Hitler and a gun with one bullet. Who do I shoot."[31] In her blog post response, Wise addressed the community to say there is nothing new about very public, incendiary criticism occurring online (or in person). Unfortunately racist and derogatory slurs and innuendos happen in a variety of spaces on our college campuses. With

continued...

LEARNING MOMENTS
(continued)

social media sites and applications, these types of incidents are amplified and need to be addressed.[32]

LESSON: Trivial issues like snow days aren't worthy of spouting digital hate online. There is little good that can come to your reputation by spreading digital hate from your accounts and apps.

· · · · ·

"If you don't like something,
change it.
If you can't change it,
change your attitude.
Don't complain."

MAYA ANGELOU

· · · · ·

Post It Forward

- You have heard the expression pay it forward: performing good deeds without expecting something in return. Digital tools like Twitter, Facebook and LinkedIn make it easy to praise someone digitally.

- Make a daily habit of posting daily a positive comment about someone via a blog, Twitter, text, Facebook or email. There are only upsides.

- Research shows that posting positive items about others increases your own happiness.[33]

- Religiously use the *Endorse, Like, Re-pin, 1+* and *Follow* buttons to make someone's day.

- When someone gives you a compliment online, reply to them with a like or favorite. Better yet, respond with a "thank you" or encouraging words.

- Social networks make it easier than ever to remember birthdays or special occasions. Make a point of writing a brief message to all your friends on their special day. It not only spreads positivity, but maintains connections with those people with whom you may only interact occasionally.

ACTION ITEM

Look for reasons to praise three people each day, expecting nothing in return. You will be amazed at the positive response you receive. We suggest taking three minutes per day to tweet about someone, endorse someone on LinkedIn, Instagram a great image of a friend and beyond.

LEARNING MOMENT

The University of Kentucky started an initiative where they crowdsourced their fans' social media support using the hashtag #WeAreUK. This is an exciting way to place fans at the center of the university's digital brand and it's a great way for the university to post it forward for their fans. Any fans that use the hashtag on Twitter or Instagram will automatically have their post show up on the #WeAreUK page on the University's website. The university is then pulling from these posts and photos to be used on physical offline billboards across the state.[34]

LESSON: As an organization look for ways to showcase and highlight your biggest advocates in special ways. In this case, it's making Kentucky fans feel special by making them bigger than life in the offline world.

LEARNING MOMENT

I loved a particular song by Christopher Tin and wanted to use it for a YouTube video I was creating. Tin embraced the idea that I was creating awareness of his music with my loyal followers. We exchanged signed copies of books for signed copies of music and posted pleasant things about one another digitally. Tin's incredible talents eventually enabled him to win two Grammy's. While we expected nothing in return by "posting it forward," each of us experienced long-term benefits.

LESSON: A one-second positive post will brighten someone's day and could brighten yours for many years to come.

• • • • •

"A life lived for others,
is the only life worth living."

ALBERT EINSTEIN

• • • • •

No. 13

Network Before You Need Your Network

- Individuals do not achieve success in a vacuum. In order to reach your goals, you need to stand on the shoulders of others. Those who succeed develop deep relationships before they need those relationships. They network before they need the network both offline and online. A candidate tracking study showed networking was the most effective method for obtaining a new job.[35]

- It's difficult to ask for a favor when you haven't communicated with or previously helped that other person.

- Online networks like LinkedIn make it easy to build new relationships or strengthen existing relationships. When you meet someone offline, cement the relationship online. It will ensure you can stay in touch in the future.

- Your fellow students now will be your co-workers and colleagues later. Do not forget to network and make connections while you're still in college. One of the easiest times to network with industry leaders is when you are a student.

- If you are a commuter student, social networking can be a great way for you to engage with and meet others on campus. Use these tools to be more involved in your college life. The dividends will pay off.

- Social media has diminished the gatekeeper to industry leaders. It's now easier than ever to reach out to your role model and receive a response.

ACTION ITEM

Once a month, make a commitment to meet with someone new for an informational interview. Informational interviews are conversations where you ask someone in your potential job field about their background, their career path and for advice about breaking into the industry. Just invite them to coffee or out for lunch and talk! A great icebreaker: I want to learn firsthand how you became such a big success after attending my university.

• • • • •

"Surround yourself with people who are smarter than you."

RUSSELL SIMMONS

• • • • •

LEARNING MOMENT

The city of Grand Rapids, Michigan was experiencing some challenging times when Newsweek wrote an article declaring it a "Dying City." In response, the entire Grand Rapids community rallied to produce the world's largest lip dub video, singing along to Don McLean's famous song "American Pie." Sponsors covered the $40,000 production cost and over 5,000 people volunteered.

The video has received millions of views and at one point was one of the Top 10 most viewed videos on YouTube. Roger Ebert called it "the greatest music video ever made."

View video here: http://bit.ly/am-pie

LESSON: ONE is never stronger than MANY, offline or online.

Praise Publicly, Criticize Privately

- Never criticize your boss, mom, teacher, rabbi or coach; the worst thing you can do is to criticize publicly, especially through digital outlets. Remember everything you say online is written in digital ink, it can't be erased.

- If you have an issue with someone, address it as quickly as possible in person. If face-to-face isn't an option, then set up a time for discussion by phone or via video conversation. Make sure your settings are set for private, not public. It is always preferable to handle conflict face-to-face.

- Sometimes our emotions get in the way of our common sense. Even the most sensible people can be caught up in the emotions of an argument with a co-worker or a negative reaction to a comment their friend made. It's often in the heat of the moment that people post things they often regret after having some time to cool down.

- If you have something positive to say about someone or something, post away! Post it forward (Rule #11).

- The company you complain about today could be your employer in the future. Think ahead to how your posts might be received.

LEARNING MOMENTS

Professors at Colgate University staged a "take back the Yak" campaign during finals week at the end of the semester. In response to a lot of negative and inflammatory posts on the Yik Yak app, they logged on and posted positive messages to their students. They wished them luck on their final assignments, wrote encouraging messages, and provided advice and support.[36]

LESSON: Social media is a tool and you have the power to influence how it is used. Organizing with others for positive change can have a supersized impact.

• • • • •

Kevin Curwick, a Minnesota High School student and football team captain, uses Twitter for good. Curwick set up the anonymous account @OsseoNiceThings to help counterattack cyberbullies. Whenever a student is attacked by cyberbullies, Curwick posts nice things about the victim to help boost that student's confidence.

The movement has been able to uplift people across the United States, Australia and England. Curwick revealed that he was the person behind the account on KARE-TV in Minneapolis-St. Paul.[37] Since this public announcement, he has since received high praise from teachers, students, potential colleges and even Ryan Seacrest. It has resulted in a "nice page" movement in other towns and cities.

LESSON: Be the link in the chain that breaks the pattern of malicious acts like cyberbullying.

Measure Twice, Post Once

- A good carpenter measures twice and cuts once. We too must read our words twice and post just once. While it may take extra time in the short term, it will save time in the long-term.

- This also can be applied to blogging. Be sure to read your posts thoroughly for grammatical and spelling errors. Even the most thoughtful posts can be ruined if they are littered with errors or incorrect data.

- According to a Jobvite Social Recruiting Survey, 93% of job recruiters reported looking at candidates' social media profiles during the job application process. 55% of recruiters have reconsidered hiring decisions based on what they have found. 66% of these recruiters reported that spelling and grammar mistakes in social posts reflected negatively on the candidate.[38]

- Short and powerful comments are usually best.

· · · · ·

"The nicest feeling in the world is to do a good deed anonymously-and have somebody find out."

OSCAR WILDE

· · · · ·

LEARNING MOMENT

Cardale Jones, a quarterback on the Ohio State University football team, made his feelings about attending classes clear on Twitter.

"Why should we have to go to class if we came here to play FOOTBALL, we ain't come to play SCHOOL classes are POINTLESS," he posted.

Embarrassed, OSU officials publicly reminded all of their athletes, "Always remember not to post or tweet anything that could embarrass themselves, their team, teammates, the university, their family or other groups, organizations or people."

Jones, a third-string quarterback at the time he tweeted this, was rushed into the national spotlight at the end of the year as a result of injuries to the two other Ohio State quarterbacks. Behind the outstanding play of Jones in the final three games, Ohio State eventually went on to be crowned National Champions. During these weeks, the media constantly mentioned this ill-advised tweet from the beginning of the season.[39]

LESSON: A respectable team member does not act selfishly. Inappropriate expressions of opinion reflect poorly on the team, whether they are shared on the field, off the field or through online outlets.

• • • • •

"In the future, we will all enjoy our 15 minutes of privacy."

SCOTT MONTY, FORD

• • • • •

The Three-Second Rule

- If you have to think for more than three seconds about whether something is appropriate—it's not.

- Read the above bullet point—then read it again!

LEARNING MOMENT

In December of 2014, a student from Georgia Tech University was indicted for hacking into the University of Georgia website. The Clarke County grand jury charged Ryan with computer trespassing, a felony, for hacking into the University's network and tampering with their online calendar. Ryan altered UGA's calendar to denote that the football team would "Get Ass Kicked by GT" on Saturday, November 29, 2014, the day of their rivalry game with Georgia Tech. Released on a $5,000 bond, Ryan faced a possible $50,000 fine and as much as 15 years in prison.[40]

LESSON: While hacking a rival's website might may seem like a harmless prank, it is actually a serious crime. Ryan now faces jail time, a huge fine, and a scar to his reputation (the first image for him on Google is his mug shot). This will likely hinder some of his employability opportunities.

LEARNING MOMENT

Nokia produced a polished television commercial for the launch of a new mobile phone. The commercial showcased the new stabilization feature of the phone's video camera.

A young, attractive couple is bike riding in Europe and the young man films the young woman as they ride. Like diet advertisements that utilize before and after photos, the commercial showcased video footage with the stabilization feature off, highlighting a bumpy ride and with the stabilization feature on, highlighting a smooth ride with clear imagery.

The smooth footage in the commercial wasn't the result of the Nokia camera. Rather, the commercial was filmed using a sophisticated high-definition movie camera mounted on a tripod in a van traveling alongside the bikes! How was Nokia caught in this deceptive act?

During the sequence, for a split second, the couple biked in front of a glass window. In that brief moment, someone slowed the video and the camera van was visible in the reflection! Nokia immediately issued a public apology and withdrew the million-dollar commercial.[41]

LESSON: Companies and teams must foster a culture of openness and encourage all staff—from junior analyst to executives—to raise a red flag when items appear untruthful or morally corrupt. Everybody benefits in an open, transparent environment.

We Will Make Digital Mistakes; How We Handle Them is What Defines Us

- It's not a question of *if* we will make an online or offline mistake, the question is when and how we handle it.

- How we handle these mistakes (with integrity) is what ultimately separates and defines our digital stamp.

- Often it's not the crime, but the cover-up that gets us into trouble (see rule #20).

- Deleting posts doesn't mean they are gone forever. Once something is posted, assume it will live on forever.

- There are many stories in this book about digital mistakes made by CEOs, students, star athletes and everyone in between. However, there are only a select few that truly illustrate how to successfully navigate those mistakes and turn them into FLAWsome moments (see rule #8). If you make a mistake online, own it and learn from it.

- The worst thing you can do after a digital mistake is leave social media all together. Don't give up, keep at it and always try to learn and improve.

LEARNING MOMENT

Married Congressman Anthony Weiner was accused of sending lewd tweets and photos to several women, including college students, while he and his wife were expecting their first child.

Weiner vehemently denied any wrongdoing and stated, "I know for a fact that my account was hacked. I can definitively say that I did not send this."[42]

Unfortunately for Weiner, a few women released to the press inappropriate photos they had received from him. One photo showcased Weiner surrounded by family photos, holding a piece of paper with the word "me" and an arrow pointing towards him. Another photo of Weiner wearing underwear was particularly damaging. Late night talk show hosts had a field day using the Congressman's last name as grist for their comedy routine.

Weiner finally admitted he hadn't been hacked. He acknowledged that he sent photos and engaged in inappropriate communication with multiple women over a three-year period. Weiner was forced to resign from Congress.

Sadly, once he was caught, he continued his inappropriate digital communication with several women. This cost him an election bid in a later campaign.

LESSON: Illicit digital acts can result in job loss and disgrace.

$$= \widehat{\underset{18}{\mathcal{N}\!o.}} =$$

Multitasking = Mistakes

- Automobile accidents often occur because one or both drivers were distracted. *Car & Driver Magazine's* research found that compared to a baseline of attentive driving, impaired drivers traveling at 70 MPH (103 feet/second) took 8 feet longer to react to danger and begin braking their vehicle. By contrast, test results showed that texting drivers took 40 feet longer to react and begin braking. Thus, the texting drivers reacted 5 times slower than the impaired drivers did.[43]

- Digital mistakes often occur because the sender was distracted. Focus on one item at a time and the potential for a digital "oops" moment is lessened. Multitaskers make up to 50% more errors.[44]

- Multiple studies demonstrate that people are healthier and more productive when they DO NOT multi-task. Neuroscience reveals that our brain doesn't have the ability to multi-task like a computer. Rather, we switch between tasks requiring our brain to decide which task is more important. Time and energy costs are associated with each of these switches.

- Put your phone away and log off social networks when you are in class or are studying. This will help you concentrate and engage in your learning.

- Know your study habits and preferences. Even though you may think you can handle distractions well, it's possible you could be doing even better.

- Neuroscientist Gary Small warns that adolescents who spend their formative years multitasking will miss out on the opportunities to for developing critical, but slow-forming interpersonal skills.[45]

ACTION ITEM

Set up or find a distraction-free study space. Then dedicate regular time each week to using this space for your schoolwork.

• • • • •

"That's been one of my mantras –
focus and simplicity. Simple can be
harder than complex: You have to work
hard to get your thinking clean to make
it simple. But it's worth it in the end
because once you get there,
you can move mountains."

STEVE JOBS

• • • • •

LEARNING MOMENT

Experts Joshua Rubinstein, PhD, Jeffrey Evans, PhD and David Meyer, PhD, estimate that switching between tasks can decrease productivity by 40 percent. Errors can result, especially if one is working on items that involve a lot of critical thinking.[46]

One in five pedestrian teenagers admitted to being distracted by their mobile device when they were treated in the emergency room after being hit by an automobile.[47]

A study by the British Institute of Psychology concluded that multi-tasking has twice the effect of smoking marijuana.[48]

LESSON: Multi-tasking makes us less efficient, more prone to make mistakes, stresses our health and can even result in serious injury.

A Picture is Worth 1,000 Words

- Photos make up 93% of the most engaging posts on Facebook[49], and with the growing popularity of social networks like Instagram, Snapchat and Pinterest, photos are quickly becoming the most popular form of social currency.

- Photos, if appropriate, can be a great way to tell your story or the story of your organization, team or school. We encourage you to use photos in your posts and find unique ways to share your story through mobile apps like Instagram and Snapchat.

- 1 in 4 individuals between the ages of 18 and 24 say they have an embarrassing photo on their phone.[50]

- Over half of Human Resource professionals that review a candidate's online reputation cite "unsuitable photos, videos and information" as a reason they reject candidates.[51]

- Here are a few key tips to keep in mind as you post and share photos online:

  - Switch off any setting that automatically syncs your photos with the cloud and consider using an offline storage method (like your hard drive or an external hard drive) for your photos.

  - Think carefully before sharing private photos with others. The receiver can easily take a screenshot or even save those photos to post at a later date. Remember, a private photo between you and your significant other or a close friend can easily be shared in the heat of an argument.

- It is a crime to share nude photos of someone else, and if that person is under the age of 18, you may be facing trafficking child pornography charges.[52]

• In general, review your privacy settings especially for networks like Facebook and Instagram where others can tag you in pictures. It may be wise to make any "tagged photos" private since many people will tag you in photos without asking your permission.

ACTION ITEM

Go back through your photo albums online. Delete, un-tag, or change the privacy settings of your photos as appropriate.

LEARNING MOMENT

Playing off the idea that selfies are selfish, students at Western Illinois University turned the concept on its head with their own "unselfie" campaign using the tag #WIUnselfie. Wanting to promote selfless acts, good deeds and other random acts of kindness, the students created Instagram and twitter accounts to post pictures of people doing positive things in the university community.[53]

LESSON: Social media can get a bad rap for encouraging self-promotional behavior, but it can also be used to promote others and causes you care about. As mentioned above, photos can tell a story about you, your organization/team, or your school. Think about how you can influence others positively and make the world a little bit more of a happy place.

• • • • •

"Honesty is the first chapter in the book of wisdom."

THOMAS JEFFERSON

• • • • •

LEARNING MOMENT

A student working at the campus recreation center at the University of Arkansas decided it would be funny to post awkward and compromising pictures of faculty and staff working out and in the locker room. He posted these to a Twitter account with captions making fun of the individuals. The student was eventually charged criminally with two counts of video voyeurism.[54]

LESSON: Although it may seem funny at the time, sometimes your posts can do harm. They may also have ramifications you have not considered. Never take secret photos or videos of others and never post these online. The consequences can be serious.

• • • • •

"Three things cannot be long hidden: the sun, the moon, and the truth."

BUDDHA

• • • • •

It's Not the Crime, But the Cover-Up

We all make mistakes and must face those online and offline mistakes head on. The next time you make a mistake:

- Own it
- Apologize
- Lay out action items and public steps to "make it right"
- Follow through on these steps
- Learn from the experience

LEARNING MOMENT

Jim Tressel, the National Champion football coach of Ohio State University, found himself in a difficult situation. His sterling reputation was under attack. Several of the team's most prominent players were accused of selling school issued memorabilia in exchange for body tattoos. Body art or tattoos are considered a form of monetary value, a direct violation of NCAA rules.

Tressel thanked the NCAA for uncovering these incidents and stated he was unaware of any such activity. Emails were later uncovered indicating Tressel had been informed of this illegal activity and did nothing to stop it. Once the emails were released, Tressel was fired for lying to the NCAA officials. In retrospect, the infractions by the players were considered minor violations and Ohio State and Tressel would have received a very light penalty had they initially acknowledged wrongdoing and asked for forgiveness. Tressel's attempt to cover-up the crime ultimately resulted in his fall from grace.[55]

LESSON: Honesty is always the best policy, especially when you make a major mistake.

Make Ginormous Public Goals

- Set goals and share them with others. When others know your goals, they are in position to support you in achieving them.

- Goals are important. Jason DeAmato, author of *For Sales*, states, "Imagine basketball without any goals. You'd simply be running around the court and passing the ball."

- I'm sure some of us have experienced this lack of focus after a long day. Make sure to hang goals at each end of your court.

Set some goals, write them down, and post them on your mirror or above your desk. Use them as a daily reminder of what you want to achieve.

ACTION ITEM

LEARNING MOMENTS

When University of San Diego student Nathan Resnick had an idea for a new type of watch buckle, he didn't just dream about it, he started a company. Nathan went on Kickstarter.com and created a crowdfunding campaign for his idea. People were so inspired by his idea and his commitment to starting a new business that he met his $15,000 campaign goal in the first three days![56] The attention continued to pour in as he reached out to any news channel and/or blog that would share his story. Nathan raised over $30,000 total on Kickstarter to fund his creative idea.[57]

LESSON: If you have a big idea, share it with the world using digital tools. You will get the support and resources you need, and you could grow your network substantially. Ultimately, it will help you achieve your goal.

· · · · ·

A child battled infant acute lymphoblastic leukemia soon after her birth. Doctors searched tirelessly to locate a bone marrow donor to match her rare blood type. After making an appeal through social media, more than 5,500 people signed up globally as potential donors. A match was eventually found in Australia.[58]

LESSON: Most people want to help others. Let them help you by publicly posting your goals. If others do not know your goals, they can't help you achieve them.

Face-2-Face Cannot Be Replaced

- 93% of communication is non-verbal. If you are spending all your time communicating via a screen, you are doing yourself a tremendous disservice.[59]

- Research indicates people are twice as likely to remember you if you shake hands. The research also shows that people with whom you shake hands will respond in a friendlier and more open manner.[60]

- 88% of people believe others are less polite on social media than in person.[61]

- Our tone in digital messages is misinterpreted 50 percent of the time.[62]

- When you are asking a professor or advisor for a letter of recommendation, always try to ask them in person. Students that ask in person and come prepared with their resume and a list of schools or jobs they are applying to will get a much better letter than those that ask online. Never ask through a Facebook message or tweet; when it comes to something as important as a letter of recommendation, face-to-face cannot be replaced.

- Developing your network requires online *and* offline interaction. Digital tools are incredible when time and distance are an issue, but you can never replace face-to-face interactions.

LEARNING MOMENT

A Mom asking one of her two daughters for help via texting:[63]

This preceding text message is funny in the sense that it's so believable. Here a mother is asking a son what the shorthand text abbreviations IDK, LY and TTYL stand for. The son provides the answers: I don't know (IDK), love you (LY) and talk to you later (TTYL). The mom believes the son is replying that he doesn't know the answer.

This is funny, but also a good reminder of how things can be easily misunderstood in text, especially from generation to generation.

LESSON: Since digital conversations lack verbal cues, it's always best to make sure you are specific and straightforward.

Tinderbox Topics—Caution!

- These subjects often cause incendiary reaction, especially within digital text where we do not have the context of non-verbal cues. When approaching these topics, use extreme caution.
  - Politics
  - Religion
- When discussing tinderbox topics, it's generally best to support your position via fact-based perspectives, rather than emotionally charged ones. To get a sense, four of the top five controversial topics on Wikipedia involve politics or religion.[64]
- Whether it is a world event that triggers an onslaught of emotionally charged social media posts, or something that has happened on campus, you want to be very thoughtful about your posts on these issues and events. Remember to be respectful, and use these times as an opportunity to practice good social media listening. Follow hashtags and peruse other posts as an opportunity to learn more about the controversy. We are a better global and campus community when there are varying viewpoints on an issue. If everyone thought exactly the same, it would be boring! Remember this, and celebrate difference in opinion among your friends, family and followers.
- News feeds and algorithms often determine the news we read and viewpoints we see. Take the time to seek out reputable alternative news sources. Step outside of the news bubble of social media.

- The best way to diffuse an argument is to agree. While you may not agree with 90% of an opposition's position, you may agree with 10%. You gain credibility with the undecided group when you acknowledge minimal agreement. This shows strength, which supports your efforts to convince the undecided group that your viewpoint has merit.

- Sometimes the best response is silence.

LEARNING MOMENT

Two different police offers were not indicted for two separate events where black men died at the hands of the officers. Many people took to both social media and the streets with their frustrations. After reading through several tweets with the hashtag #BlackLivesMatter a police officer in San Jose, Phillip White, posted hateful tweets on his personal Twitter account. One tweet read, "By the way if anyone feels they can't breathe or their lives matter I'll be at the movies tonight, off duty, carrying my gun." This along with other inappropriate tweets that White posted resulted in his suspension without pay. A change.org petition started urging the police station to fire him. Subsequently, White lost his job as a coach at Menlo College. A representative from Menlo posted on their Facebook wall that they would not associate with someone that expresses bigotry.[65]

LESSON: Sharing extreme or intolerant opinions will hurt your digital reputation and negatively impact other areas of your life. You are always a representation of your employer, student organization or team (see rule #31). Be especially deliberate and thoughtful when engaging in digital conversations involving "Tinderbox Topics."

LEARNING MOMENT

SECRET SERVICE BORED: A member of the secret service mistakenly thought he was posting to his own Twitter account, but instead his disapproval of Fox News went out on behalf of the entire secret service: "Had to monitor Fox for a story. Can't. Deal. With. The. Blathering."[66]

LESSON: Know your professional position and understand that while your friends may post something on a particular topic, you may not have this same luxury based on your job, position, team or company.

· · · · ·

"Fear less, hope more, eat less, chew more, whine less, breathe more, talk less, say more, hate less, love more, and good things will be yours."

SWEDISH PROVERB

· · · · ·

The Power of a Letter

- How do you feel when you receive another email? How do you feel when you receive a handwritten letter in the mail? A nice handwritten letter makes your day. Make someone's day.

- In our world of tweeting, texting and emailing, a letter will get you noticed. Be unique. Stand out. Personally written paper notes are in decline. According to a U.S. Postal Service's survey, the average home in 1987 received a personal letter *once every two weeks* and now it's *once every seven weeks* and declining. Whereas the average business e-mail account sends and receives over 100 e-mails daily and the younger generation sends over 100 texts daily.[67]

- Next time you make a mistake, take the time to send a letter. It is significantly more personal than email and shows that you truly care.

- Did you just complete a really exciting internship with a company you would like to work for after graduation? Send your supervisor a handwritten letter explaining why you loved your job. This will make their day, and it will help you stand out and build your network before you need it (see rule # 13).

ACTION ITEM

Who is someone you have not spoken with in a while? Is there a colleague that helped you with a project at work? A coach who was instrumental in your long-term success? Identify someone in your life and reach out to him or her with a letter or card.

LEARNING MOMENT

When Ohio State quarterback J.T. Barrett suffered a season ending ankle injury, he received some support from an unsuspecting source – his archrival. The University of Michigan quarterback, Devin Gardner, rushed over from his sideline to the prone Barrett. A picture of the two rival quarterbacks went viral online. Upon seeing the photo, the Ohio State Athletic Director sent a letter of thanks to Gardner. Gardner posted a picture of the letter on social media, expressing his thanks to the OSU Athletic Director.[68]

LESSON: Sportsmanship always wins, no matter what. In addition, a letter can be much more powerful than any other kind of communication (besides face to face). While OSU could have easily shared a nice post on social media, it meant much more to Garnder that they took the time to send him a letter. When you want to show someone you care, send a letter.

LEARNING MOMENT

A CEO of a Fortune 500 company invited me to deliver a keynote to a room full of Fortune 1000 CEOs. I was so grateful that I sent a handwritten thank you note. My wife and I also sent his family a Christmas card.

Several months later, I received a call from the Dean at the McCombs School of Business asking me to deliver the commencement address to that year's graduating MBA class. I was surprised and delighted. It was an honor to return to the Austin campus where I had received my MBA. This incredible opportunity seemed to come from nowhere. I learned later that I was strongly recommended by that Fortune 500 CEO.

LESSON: You will never regret taking the time to write someone a personal letter... on paper.

Cyberbullying: Don't Enable It

- Cyberbullying is defined as teasing, insulting or making fun of another person online. The intent is often to soil the target's reputation. If you are a cyberbully, STOP! Your bullying could be the byproduct of social anxiety or low self-esteem and it is important that you seek help. Teachers, friends, parents and school counselors are increasingly aware of the signs of cyberbullying and will eventually confront you. Cyberbullying is often considered a criminal offense and offline bullying laws apply to online behavior.

- Cyberbullies leave digital fingerprints and often are easier to prosecute than traditional bullies who do not leave as much incriminating evidence.

- Bullying can ultimately lead to a victim's suicide. Victims of cyberbullying are twice as likely to commit suicide as those who have not had a cyberbullying experience.

- 1 in 4 teens report that they have experienced repeated bullying via their cell or on the internet.[69]

- Over half of all teens that use social media have witnessed outright bullying online, and an astounding 95 percent of teens who witness bullying on social media have ignored the behavior.[70] We all must serve as upstanders and not bystanders to cyberbullying.

- Colleges and universities have their own rules and procedures for dealing with cyber-bullying, cyber-harassment, and cyber-stalking. If you know something that is occurring, tell a faculty or staff member. They can help and give you options.

- Being harassed or bullied online can be mentally draining. Reach out to others to help you process through it. The counseling services on your campus can also help.

LEARNING MOMENT

Phoebe Prince, a 15-year-old high school student from Massachusetts, was harassed by a group of "mean girls" for dating a senior within her first few weeks of her freshman year. Not only did they harass and threaten her at school, the girls would cyberbully her by calling her obscene names on Twitter, Craigslist, Facebook and Formspring.

Prince, unable to take the threats, went home from school and hung herself in a stairwell. Her bullies did not stop there; they continued to post mean comments on her Facebook memorial page. Seven teens were convicted of several crimes including: criminal harassment, stalking and civil rights violations.[71]

LESSON: Words are powerful and can be very hurtful. When one is hidden behind a screen they can sometimes feel more confident to say things they would never say to someone offline. Cyberbullying can result in suicide; don't be a cyberbully and don't enable it.

LEARNING MOMENT

Natalie Farzaneh, a high school student, became a victim of cyberbullying after getting a Facebook and Formspring account. Through these social media accounts, people would message her telling her to commit suicide and that the world would be better off without her. These messages led her to suicidal thoughts and ultimately self-harming.

Farzaneh turned her abuse into a way to work as an advocate for surviving these cyber-bullies. As a 15-year-old, she works as a mentor for the beat bullying program called Cyber Mentoring. She also works as a motivational speaker for different schools.

Paige Chandler, a cyberbullying victim, was attacked via Formspring. People would send her anonymous comments insulting her appearance calling her "ugly and fat."

At the age of 17, she also has joined CyberMentor.org.uk to help other victims of online abuse.[72]

LESSON: Anyone, old and young, can stand up and fight evil.

Be a Digital Change Agent

- Digital tools like Kickstarter and Indiegogo allow ideas from students for come to life. These free platforms enable you to receive the funding from fans, fellow students, friends and just about anyone who believes in your idea.

- On campus, students are using digital tools to create change in several ways. Whether it be a petition on Change.org or a hashtag they use to connect with other students interested in joining the cause, students are leveraging digital tools to change their campus and the world.

- Research indicates Millennials (those born between 1980 and 1999) are the most generous and socially conscious generation yet.[73]

- Governments and elected leaders are increasingly reaching out directly to their citizens and constituents. In the United States, The White house began "We The People" at *petitions.whitehouse.gov* to allow for more participatory democracy. Petitions receiving 100,000 signatories in the first 30 days automatically receive a response from the President.[74]

Visit *Change.org* and *Kickstarter.com* to see how these digital tools are helping people all over the world create change in their community.

**ACTION
ITEM**

LEARNING MOMENT

A young woman contacted her sister after falling victim to domestic violence. She called her sister that night to tell her that she was rushed to the emergency room after her boyfriend beat her. Her sister came to pick her up and get her to a safe place, but there was only one problem. The boyfriend and the victim shared a cell phone plan, and for as long as they were under the same plan, her abusive boyfriend had access to all of her phone records and would know who she was calling and where she was calling from. When she called Verizon to cancel the plan, they gave her the standard response letting her know that it would cost her $500 to cancel her plan.

Her sister didn't believe this was just or fair, so she did something about it. She went to Change.org to petition for this rule to change. After the petition received nearly 200,000 signatures, the victim's sister received a personal phone call from Verizon Wireless. They apologized for their policy, and made changes to that policy and the training they provided to their customer service agents dealing with customers that have become victims of domestic violence. In addition, they started a new initiative where their customer service agents cannot only help victims cancel their plans, but they will also connect them to additional resources for domestic violence.[75]

LESSON: Digital tools like *Change.org* can be used to connect people and rally for a cause. Also, kudos to Verizon Wireless for following rule #8, be FLAWsome, and improving their current systems and policies to better serve victims of violence.

LEARNING MOMENT

As a West Virginia University first year student, Carrie Shade decided she was going to take action and help those dealing with mental illness. After losing a close friend to suicide the year before, she came to realize that 1 in 4 people between the ages of 18 and 24 deal with mental illness. Shade started a Twitter handle @AgainstSuicide to help other young people dealing with mental illness. She uses the handle to post inspiring messages, and connects with those having a hard time to share an uplifting message.[76]

LESSON: Use digital tools for social good. You no longer have to be a person of note to make a massive difference, digital tools allow you to create change and positively impact others at any age.

Be Genuine

- There is only one you. Be yourself. Be genuine.

- Often a perceived weakness can be a bridge to a deeper connection. For example if you are afraid of heights and someone else is afraid of heights, you share something in common that you can connect through and openly discuss and assist one another.

- Being open and genuine is how you learn. The more open you are, the more opportunities that will come to you. The energy you put out into the world is the energy you will receive back.

- It's easy to get caught up in the appearances of others. Social media tends to amplify the positive and omit the negative. If you constantly compare yourself to others, you will miss out on what is positive in your own life.

- Don't "humblebrag." Humblebragging is posting a comment that seems humble but really serves to boast about something in your life. *Example:* "I can't believe I applied to eight Ivy League institutions and only got admitted to three of them."

- Don't engage in tricks or games just to get people to like your posts or follow you. Focus on good content and they will follow. Your goal should be connection, not affirmation.

- Customers reward businesses that are open and authentic. According to the ALOFT Group, a study by Napoli, et al., found that brand authenticity is a better predictor of purchase intentions than brand love, trust or credibility.[77]

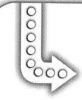 **ACTION ITEM**

Review your social media accounts. Are they representing the real you?

LEARNING MOMENTS

In 2014, Facebook changed the options for listing one's gender on the social network. Profiles now include the ability for one to select which pronouns the site will use to identify the user and choose from 50 different gender designations. Users can list one or multiple within their profiles, including terms such as "transgender" or "intersex." These profile changes have made the site more inclusive of people of different identity expressions.[78]

LESSON: Social networks can be a great avenue for self-expression and exploration. Sometimes we are limited by the way the network was designed, but there are infinite possibilities for exploring who we are and who we want to be.

• • • • •

In January of 2014, a post-graduate student Noorulann Shahid started the hashtag #lifeofamuslimfeminist to discuss the complexities of being a Muslim feminist. She says that using the hashtag was never meant to start a movement, but it did. Many other Muslim women jumped at the chance to tell their story using the hashtag.

"White feminists argue women should be able to dress how they want to, yet refuse to let me wear my hijab in peace #lifeofamuslimfeminist."

Above is an example of one of the many tweets that referenced the hashtag and ultimately helped to tell the story of Muslim feminists. Noorulann was featured in the Huffington Post and is credited for opening up a very important dialogue around achieving feminism in an intercultural and more inclusive way.[79]

LESSON: With the use of Twitter, students can start international conversations about important issues. When you are genuine online you inspire people to share their story and be authentic both on and offline.

$$\equiv \left(\begin{array}{c} \mathcal{N}o. \\ 28 \end{array}\right) \equiv$$

Fail Fast, Fail Forward, Fail Better

- As entrepreneurs, individuals or organizations, the rapid pace of digital expansion means that our initiatives might fail the first time. In fact, failure may result more frequently than success.

- The fastest way to increase our rate of learning in the digital era is to increase our rate of failure.

- Failing better is the ability to detect when a construct just isn't right for the current situation. Successful people know how to pivot an idea or business plan quickly. They pivot toward something that may prove more successful than their original plan. For example, 3Ms Post-It Notes were the result of a failed glue design.

- A recent survey by American Express showed the top three characteristics of "influencers" are: 1) Confidence 2) Education 3) The willingness to try new things. Go ahead, try new things and do not worry about failing.[80]

LEARNING MOMENT

Wine and liquor storeowner Gary Vaynerchuk of the Wine Library had 12 people watch his first YouTube wine show. These viewers believed the format was stuffy and traditional and encouraged him to take advantage of his outgoing New Jersey personality and develop a more entertaining format. Gary listened to his fan base. The Wine Library became one of the most viral shows on YouTube and sales increased from $3 million annually to $45 million[81] and then over $50 million. Gary is now a bestselling author, media company owner and keynote speaker.

LESSON: Don't easily give up on a good idea if it doesn't work the first time. It might eventually make you $50 million dollars.

• • • • •

"You can't build a reputation on what you are going to do."

HENRY FORD

• • • • •

Freedom of Choice—
Not Freedom From Consequence

- Despite our loss of privacy, we still have the freedom of choice. You may tattoo the devil on your forehead but limit your ability to secure employment, a significant consequence.

- Our online and offline choices impact our employer, family, friends, everyone. These choices often determine whether we are hired or fired, liked or disliked, promoted or demoted.

LEARNING MOMENT

A student at a Michigan university posted a vague anonymous message online that read, "I'm gonna (pistol symbol) the school at 12:15 p.m. today." Campus police initiated a campus wide lockdown and worked with internet service providers to track the message. Police arrived at the student's residence hall room and the student now faces 20 years in prison for making a terrorist threat or false report of terrorism. The threat was posted and then immediately taken it down by the student, but the damage was done.[82]

LESSON: Authorities take online threats seriously. Even though you may immediately remove a post after you make it, it can still have an impact. You will be held accountable by authorities for your online actions.

LEARNING MOMENT

When Evan Wilder was knocked from his bike by a reckless car, he was more concerned with his life than getting the license plate of the hit-and-run driver. Witnesses were unavailable. However, the video camera that Wilder had affixed to his bike helmet proved helpful. After watching the video recording, police were able to locate and apprehend the guilty driver.[83]

LESSON: We have choices. Will we lift someone up or knock someone down?

• • • • •

You take unacceptable risk, you have to be prepared to face the consequence.

CARLY FIORINA

• • • • • •

No. 30

Join Your Campus Community Online

- Follow your college's main social media accounts. These will give you timely information about deadlines to look out for and major events on campus. Also, in the event of an emergency, these are often some of the channels schools use to get the word out.

- When you're admitted to college, join your "Class of" groups and participate with your class' hashtag. Even before you get to campus, you can begin making friends and meeting people.

- Participate in social media at new student orientation. Social media is being used more and more in orientation. Perhaps the staff is running a photo contest or a scavenger hunt. These are great ways to get to know the campus and your fellow students.

- Your college campus is a community, and in the digital age, that community is not something that exists within the physical "walls" surrounding your campus; it extends online. Participating in the conversation online in a positive way is an excellent way to build relationships on campus.

- Just remember, face-to-face cannot be replaced (see rule #22) so eventually you will need to go to organization meeting or community service event to bond with fellow students. However, for those that are a little shy, connecting online at first can help you feel more comfortable putting yourself out there on campus.

LEARNING MOMENT

The brothers of Beta Mu Chapter of Delta Sigma Phi at Transylvania University recorded a lip dub video of Taylor Swift's song, *Shake It Off*. The video went viral and demonstrated how Greek life can contribute to community, collaboration, and leadership. The video was even noticed by Taylor Swift herself who tweeted, "I'm personally inviting all of these guys (and a date!) to a show on tour next year, it's on me. Nailed it, bros!"[84]

LESSON: Your school, team or student organization can use digital tools to propel you into a level of success you may have never dreamed of! Social media can be a powerful tool for promoting a group or organization's message. You never know who will see it or the effects it may have.

• • • • •

"Associate with men of good quality if you esteem your own reputation; for it is better to be alone than in bad company."

GEORGE WASHINGTON

• • • • •

No. 31

You Represent Your School, Organizations, Team & Family

- The ability to have separate personalities and behaviors for your work life versus your private life no longer exists. This shift is permanent and we need to embrace new challenges and opportunities.

- Positive and negative choices not only impact your digital reputation, but also your company, co-workers, church, family...everyone with whom you associate.

- The world has shifted. It is now interconnected and your actions may have unintended consequences.

- When you're a leader on campus, you live in a fishbowl. Student teams, clubs and organizations are public and closely watched. Even as an individual, you will be looked at as if you speak for your group.

- Visible campus student leaders are held to an even higher standard than their peers. If you hold a major leadership office or role, surround yourself with other leaders who can help hold you accountable.

LEARNING MOMENTS

A Columbia University football player was charged with a hate crime for an alleged assault of an Asian student. A local news outlet investigated the tweets of the football team and uncovered numerous sexist, racist, and homophobic comments. The revelation led to questions about the culture of the entire football program and the behaviors of all of the athletes.[85]

LESSON: Racist, sexist, and homophobic attitudes and posts are never appropriate. Your online posts can come back to haunt you and can have an impact on your teammates, your team, and your school.

• • • • •

A social fraternity at the University of Pennsylvania posted a group holiday photo to their Facebook account. The students, largely white, decided to pose with dark-skinned blow up doll sex toy. The picture immediately received national attention and the NAACP released a statement. The Interfraternity Council disciplined the group and their international organization also took action. The fraternity ultimately apologized.[86]

LESSON: When in a student club or organization, it is everyone's responsibility to be mindful of group action. It is on you to stand up when you see something wrong or could be viewed as inappropriate before it is too late.

• • • • •

Comedian Gilbert Gottfried started tweeting jokes about Japan right after tens of thousands were killed by the 2011 Tsunami. It cost him his job as the voice of the Aflac duck.[87]

LESSON: Digital sarcasm focusing on catastrophic events is always unwise. Your postings have the power to help or harm those with whom you associate.

No. 32

Be a Baker, not an Eater

- Because of the stress and fast-paced nature of today's world, as a survival instinct, we often will take on an internal focus. This internal focus often looks like this: *What do I need to get done? What is this activity doing for me?* However, if we all take the time *to be kinder than we need to be,* not only will we make the world a better place, but we will start to see others help us more too.

- As author Guy Kawasaki stresses, be a *Baker*, not an *Eater.* A baker understands that more pies can always be made. An *Eater* upon seeing someone else eat a slice a pie immediately thinks, *"Hey, there will be less for me...I better eat as much pie as I can now."*

· · · · ·

"Character is like a tree and reputation like a shadow. The shadow is what we think of it; the tree is the real thing."

ABRAHAM LINCOLN

· · · · ·

LEARNING MOMENTS

As a sophomore at Swarthmore, Aditi Kulkarni is empowering women on campus and around the world with the Red Lips Project Tumblr blog. Kulkarni wanted to create a digital space where women could share what makes them feel powerful. She explains on the blog's About page, "Women are intrinsically powerful. But I realized that many of the women in my life don't always have a space to express their power. I wanted to create a project to change this and give them that space." The Red Lips Project has been a huge success and Kulkarni plans to expand it to colleges around the country. Here are a few examples of the entries that have been posted by women on the Red Lips Project:

"What makes me feel powerful is believing in my own decisions."

"I feel powerful when bringing happiness to others."

"What makes me feel powerful is the ability to turn ideas into actualizations."[88]

LESSON: Digital tools like Tumblr are great to create a community and solicit submissions from fans. Follow Kulkarni's lead, and if you recognize an opportunity to empower others then go for it and create it!

LEARNING MOMENT

An airline gate attendant was curt with passengers, and in some instances, rude. It was obvious she didn't want to be working. In return for her unpleasantness, people posted negative comments online about the airline service and her unprofessional behavior.

An elderly woman in front of me kindly said to her, "Listen dear, I know something else must be bothering you." Tears rolled down the attendant's face when she sobbed, "It's my little boy. He is very sick and in the children's hospital. My husband is so distressed that he can't work at his construction job so I have to work extra hours here to help pay the medical bills, when I should be taking care of my son." From there, customers and co-workers within hearing distance were sympathetic and shifted their attitudes to help the gate attendant positively in her time of distress.

LESSON: Always try to see everyone in the best light. The healthy do not require a helping hand or to be healed. The weak and the sick need help. Anger is often an outward manifestation of pain or sadness.

Your Legacy =
Digital Footprint + Digital Shadows

- 92% of children under the age of two have a digital shadow. Sonograms are also posted to social media even before kids are born![89]

- Digital Footprint = items you upload about yourself.

- Digital Shadow = items that others post about you.

- Digital Stamp = the summary of information people will learn about you today and 300 years from now digitally, your digital legacy. Digital Stamp = Digital Footprints + Shadows.

- Digital Trail = Your actions, shopping habits and searches online that are captured by companies through cookies or data files in your browser. You have a digital trail even though you may not even know what is in it.

· · · · ·

"Your reputation is in the hands of others. That's what a reputation is. You can't control that. The only thing you can control is your character."

WAYNE W. DYER

· · · · ·

ACTION ITEM

Take a moment to research your Digital Stamp. Opt out of website tracking when possible and remove old posts.

LEARNING MOMENT

Whitney Kropp, a Michigan high school student, was the victim of a cruel prank. As a joke, her classmates voted to include her to be on homecoming court. At the encouragement of her family, Kropp held her head high, faced her bullies and remained on the court.

News of the prank spread and local residents rallied behind Kropp. Businesses donated a homecoming dress, shoes and free salon styling. A Facebook page in her honor was created and received over 100,000 likes from around the globe.

"It is absolutely awesome to see her stand up," beamed her mother, Bernice Kropp. "And it's so cool to see e-mails ... we're getting from parents and other students from all over the place telling her stories and how it helped them and it touched them. My daughter is out there as an inspiration to a lot of people, and it's a really cool thing."[90] Whitney posted a video on YouTube to thank her supporters and it went viral.

LESSON: Often the best way to combat a negative force is to stand up to that force and shine a light on it.

No. 34

Surround yourself with success

- A critical item to success is to surround oneself with the right people both offline and online (for online, we strongly suggest LinkedIn). 15% of the reason a person gets a job, keeps a job, or advances in a job is related to technical skills and job knowledge; 85% has to do with people skills.[91]

- Remind your supporters how important and valued they are to you by giving them digital hugs and digital bouquets—do not forget the real hugs and flowers either!

- Pay attention to cues from your support network regarding what you do well and what you do poorly. Take advantage of your career development resources and staff. Setup a meeting and ask if you can have ongoing assessment and feedback on your strengths and weaknesses.

- At the beginning of our college careers, we often surround ourselves with individuals out of convenience (roommates, orientation groups, etc.), but as we progress, we begin to find our way and choose our friends. Who do you want to get to know? Where do you need to put yourself to meet these people?

ACTION ITEM

Reflect on your friend groups. Are they reflective of you? Should you continue to befriend these individuals or find new ones?

LEARNING MOMENT

Seven-year-old Jack Hoffman lived a dream when he was called onto the Nebraska Huskers' football field. Dressed in football pads and a little red Nebraska football jersey, Jack made a symbolic 69-yard touchdown run. The play became the Video of the Week on ESPN and it received over eight million YouTube views. President Obama even paid Jack a personal visit.

You see, Jack was diagnosed with pediatric brain cancer in April of 2011 and undergone multiple surgeries and chemotherapy.[92] Rex Burkhead, Nebraska's running back, became fast friends with Jack. Burkhead, Captain of "Team Jack," was instrumental in getting Jack on the field for his historic run. Sixty thousand fans stood and cheered as loud as they do for their National Championship Teams. It was a day Jack will never forget.

Burkhead said after the emotional run, "Jack is a fighter, a strong kid. To see him run around and enjoy the Husker experience, it's a dream come true, especially for kids in the state of Nebraska. For Jack to get down here and do it, I know it made his day." Jack said that the moment "felt awesome."[93]

continued...

LEARNING MOMENTS
(continued)

The Nebraska football team understood Jack needed a lift and in giving him one, Jack, in turn, lifted the spirits of a nation.

Watch video of Jack's run: http://bit.ly/1Eh45Cp

LESSON: By doing well for one, you can positively impact millions when compelling stories spread virally through digital and traditional media.

• • • • •

"Surround yourself with only people who are going to lift you higher."

OPRAH WINFREY

• • • • •

Watch Your Language

- Have you ever said, "Man I wished I should have used foul language in my last post or used the f#$% word." No, but certainly the reverse is true. I wish I hadn't used that particular word. Words matter.

- Hateful words or phrases can be as damaging as obscene ones. If you wouldn't be comfortable wearing it as a T-shirt around the people that you reference, then do not post it online.

- With the rise of campus shootings, Campus Police are now being trained to look for inflammatory comments both offline and online. The police will error on the side of caution – "I was just joking" isn't a solid defense for your inflammatory language. To that point, "I'm going to kill you" is no longer appropriate or accepted slang when posting online or even offline.

LEARNING MOMENT

Six Nevada teenagers in middle school were arrested for posting and sending "Attack A Teacher Day."

One girl was arrested for sending the original post to over one hundred people and five others were arrested for responding with graphic details on which teacher they'd like to attack and what they would do to them.

The girls were surprised that they were subsequently arrested. They stated it was simply a joke.

"School shootings really happen. That's why we took it seriously. It's not OK, and it's not funny in this day and age if you're going to make a threat against a teacher," said Carson Middle School Principal, Dan Sadler.[94]

LESSON: Threats in digital context are no joking matter. Digital words matter.

• • • • •

"Things do not change; we change."

HENRY DAVID THOREAU

• • • • •

Teach & Train Your Fellow Students, Friends & Family

- When your fellow students, friends or family members post something digitally, this will have a direct negative or positive reflection on them and you.

- If you are a part of a student organization, suggest that training include a speaker or educational session on how to act online as both an individual and as a group. During a retreat or at the beginning of the year, have a conversation with your group as to how you will handle social media.

- Fool me once, shame on me; fool me twice, shame on you. When something negative occurs, you have nobody to blame but yourself, since you didn't take the time to teach and train your team, employees or family. A great first step is to give them this book. By helping others, you are ultimately helping yourself.

LEARNING MOMENT

A Massachusetts high school teacher was fired for posting on Facebook, "I'm so not looking forward to another year at Cohasset Schools," she added that the community was "arrogant" and "snobby."

"I made a stupid mistake with my Facebook post, it may have cost me my career," she said.[95]

LESSON: If you fail to train your teachers, employees or team how to use social media properly, it may result in you having to terminate an otherwise positive contributor.

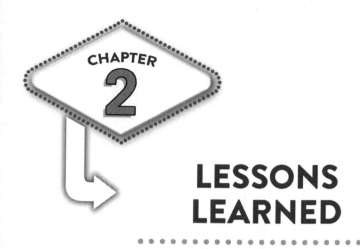

LESSONS LEARNED

Lessons Learned in Careers

Lying employee gets caught...in a tutu

A U.S. employee of Anglo-Irish Bank asked his boss for a personal day to address a family matter. Someone then posted the employee's photo on Facebook. He was in attendance at a party holding a wand and wearing a tutu. All his colleagues discovered the lie.[96]

LESSON: Don't lie to your boss. Whether you post the picture or you're tagged in one, it's very easy to get caught in a lie. Be truthful, always.

• • • • •

Facebook CEO posts damage his reputation

Facebook CEO Mark Zuckerberg has made some costly missteps as they relate to his reputation. Among them, he made negative comments to a friend that came across as conniving and backstabbing toward early developers of a Facebook-like social network.

Friend: so have you decided what you are going to do about the websites?

Zuck: yea i'm going to $%@k them

In another exchange leaked to Silicon Valley Insider, Zuckerberg explained to a friend that his control of Facebook gave him access to any information he wanted on any Harvard student:

Zuck: yea so if you ever need info about anyone at harvard

Zuck: just ask

Zuck: i have over 4000 emails, pictures, addresses, sns

Friend: what!? how'd you manage that one?

Zuck: people just submitted it

Zuck: i don't know why

Zuck: they "trust me"4

Zuck: dumb $%@ks[97]

LESSON: If one of the best technological minds in the world, Mark Zuckerberg, can make a digital mistake, then it can happen to anyone.

• • • • •

#ChevyGuy [FLAWsome]

Chevrolet executive Rikk Wilde's poor delivery of a brand new Chevrolet Colorado Truck went viral and for all the wrong reasons. We would think poor Mr. Wilde, poor Chevrolet right? We would be wrong. Immediately following this nationally televised gaffe, traffic to the truck's website dramatically increased, as did sales for the truck. But why and how is this possible? It's all about being FLAWsome. Let me explain.

First we need to start with why Wilde was on television rather than one of Chevrolet's top executives. Wilde is Chevrolet's zone manager for Kansas City, and a lifelong Royals fan. The Royals had an 80% chance of winning game seven and clinching the World Series Baseball title. Chevrolet thought it would be neat if the Royals did indeed win that it would be Wilde presenting the Most Valuable Player (MVP) of the World Series with the truck.

Well, not only did the Royals lose game seven, but Wilde appeared overwhelmed by the moment when he was presenting the truck to the MVP of the San Francisco Giants. Sweating profusely and fumbling his words, Wilde lost track of the script he had on crumbled notes clenched in his sweaty palm. He had to go from memory on describing the features of the truck. At one point stammering, "Uhhh... it has technology and stuff."

The Twittersphere immediately started using hashtags #ChevyGuy and #TechnologyAndStuff. Many posters were indicating it was like a Chris Farley SNL skit.

When the less-than-polished presentation became an instant media sensation, GM realized "we could ride the wave or get dragged down by it," Chevrolet spokesman Mike Albano said. So the company embraced it.

Immediately following the awkward delivery, Jamie Barbout of the Chevrolet social media team began tweeting this from the ChevyTrucks account:

> "Truck yeah the 2015 #ChevyColorado has awesome #TechnologyAndStuff!"

GM even started using the #technologyandstuff hashtag and included it in a press release touting the new mid-size pickup.

The nervous Wilde was assured by his boss he still had a job as a zone manager, working with dealers. "This elevated his status to uber-hero," said Albano. The Chevrolet brand received over $2.4 million in media exposure from the unconventional presentation (according to Front Row Analytics).[98] Bloomberg reports this is six times more than the $392,000 it would have brought in with a more polished performance. Most importantly, Chevrolet.com website saw a 70% hike in visitors.

The SEC ESPN Network tweeted:

> "Here at the SEC Network we run on #technologyandstuff."

Mark Reuss, president of GM North America, tweeted:

> "It's what I've been saying for years.....#technologyandstuff."[99]

LESSON: As an educator or student, you might not find yourself in the national spotlight, but there may be times when you have a "Wilde" like moment. When you have your gaffe, don't run from it. Embrace it like Chevrolet.

• • • • •

Racists getting fired

The editor of the Tumblr blog "Racists Getting Fired" actively looks for people on Twitter and other social media channels that are posting racist remarks.

They take a screenshot of the status and post the picture on "Racists Getting Fired." With the help of their Tumblr followers they track down the employers of the individuals that post racist and hurtful messaging so that the employer can also see what is being posted online. In one instance, they identified a young man that was using foul and derogatory language towards African Americans. This individual had several racist posts. He used a screen name for his handle instead of his real name, making it tricky to track down his employer. However, after looking closely at the individual's tweet history, they came across the following tweet with his full name.

Once they had his full name, the bloggers looked him up on Facebook and tracked down his employer. Shortly after they sent these screenshots to his employer, the individual tweeted out an apology and told his followers that he was suspended without pay for his actions.[100]

LESSON: Hurtful and derogatory language is never appropriate. Your employer has the right to suspend or fire you if your social media reflects poorly upon them.

· · · · ·

Student uses Twitter to land on the set of a Netflix documentary

Nikki Uy decided it was time to improve her digital reputation. She started by creating an About.me page and Twitter account. She was home on break and binge watching some Netflix, when she stumbled upon a documentary series called Shelter Me. The show features new stories in each episode about shelter animals that get adopted and go on to live happy lives. Nikki sent the show a Tweet letting them know how the show inspired her. Interested in production and film, Nikiki also offered to help. Her tweets eventually turned into e-mails and phone calls with the show and she was invited to volunteer at a live filming on the set. She had an incredible experience and met some talented producers.[101]

LESSON: There no longer is a gatekeeper standing in the way of your dreams or the people you want to meet. You can use social media to connect with people in your industry, find experiences that will build your resume, and connect with a network before you need it. Use social media to build your network and connect with industry leaders.

• • • • •

Tim Armstrong AOL CEO fires employee on conference call

Tim Armstrong, CEO of AOL, fired an employee during a conference call. Abel Lenz, Armstrong's Creative Director, reportedly tried to take a photo of Armstrong during the meeting concerning cutbacks. According to TechCrunch, a website owned by AOL, Armstrong said, "Abel, put that camera down. You're fired." Minutes later, Armstrong said, "The reason I fired Abel is I don't want anyone taking pictures of this meeting."[102]

LESSON: Leaders need to understand they need to watch their words and actions as they are being broadcast. If Armstrong had to do it again, he probably would have said, "Abel, you are dismissed from this meeting." Then later, he could fire him.

• • • • •

LG's mockery of iPhones backfires

LG attempted to poke fun at Apple's #bendgate by tweeting from their LG France account "Our smartphones don't bend, they are naturally curved ;)." LG looked foolish when it was discovered they had tweeted from an iPhone, not an LG.[103]

LESSON: If you as an employee are going to take on another company or organization you are best served making certain everything on your end is a clean as possible. Since none of us are 100% perfect it's probably best to not engage in this type of behavior in the first place – rather spend time showcasing your merits rather than pointing out someone else's warts.

• • • • •

Carl Icahn tweet sends Apple stock soaring

It's been called the "Tweet heard round the world." On August 13, 2013, Carl Icahn sent out a tweet that increased the stock price of Apple by 3% in minutes. His tweet read, "We currently have a large position in APPLE. We believe the company to be extremely undervalued. Spoke to Tim Cook today. More to come."[104]

Icahn has yet to disclose how much he invested in Apple, but CNBC reported his stake being worth over $2 billion. Almost immediately after the tweet, the stock's market capitalization increased $10 billion.

LESSON: Social media messages can have dynamic impacts on financial markets.

• • • • •

Woman fired before she's even hired

A young woman was happy to receive a job offer from Cisco. Not sure whether to take the job she posted on Twitter, "Cisco just offered me a job! Now I have to weigh the utility of a fatty paycheck against the daily commute to San Jose and hating the work." The company revoked the offer tweeting: "Who is the hiring manager? I'm sure they would love to know you will hate the work. We here at Cisco are versed in the Web."[105]

LESSON: Saying negative comments about your current or future job has negative consequences.

• • • • •

Twitter being used to cast movie stars

Twitter is now being used as a way to cast movies. President of global revenue at Twitter, Adam Bain, refers to it as a "Moneyball-style" approach to find actors. The actors are being considered because of their follower count as well as their engagement via social media with their fans.[106]

• • • • •

NJ faculty members faces
major repercussions after racist posts

A New Jersey area adjunct professor is facing allegations of racism and potentially losing her job at multiple colleges. Nancy Reeves, who teaches sociology courses at Widener University, Rowan University, and Rowan College at Glouces-ter County, is under fire for re-posting racially charged content on Facebook. Reeves reposted approximately twenty images from "Mexican Word of the Day," which parodies dic-tionary entries. One such post depicted a sizeable man wearing a sombrero with a supposed Mexican accent stating: "Asbestos. I did jur [sic] lawn asbestos I could."

The posts were made available to the media and to the colleges where Reeves teaches by a former student in January of 2015. Reeves, who has "unfriended" all current and former students from her Facebook page, now faces allegations of racial bias impacting how she has made grading decisions in her courses, which she denies.[107]

LESSON: Posting or re-posting digital content can be easily construed as endorsement. The decision to post insensitive content on a personal website is now the basis for questioning this faculty member's professional judgment and decisions. The outcome of each of these universities investigations into this matter will impact her career, her ability to be hired by other institutions, and leaves all of her previous grade assignments under scrutiny.

· · · · ·

Justin Bieber: From the streets to the Grammy's via YouTube

One of the most famous YouTube success stories is Justin Bieber. Throughout his tween years, his mother would post videos of Justin singing on YouTube. After a while, people took notice of this talented youngster. A Marketing Executive, Scooter Braun, then pursued Justin in hopes to represent him. At only 13 years old, Bieber recorded a demo and performed for hip-hop artist Usher who signed him to Raymond Braun Media Group.

Justin Bieber grew his net worth to $200 million and sold over 15 million albums and hundreds of sold out shows.[108] He is the most-followed person on Twitter with more followers then the populations of countries including Germany, Turkey, South Africa, Canada, Argentina and Egypt. Justin Bieber has YouTube (and his mother) to thank for all of this incredible fame and fortune.

Lessons Learned: Personal & Family

Divorce due to Snapchat photos

A married man went out with some friends who encouraged him to create a Tinder account, a dating app where people can swipe through photos of eligible singles nearby to find a date. As the night went on and he connected with some of the single women he met on Tinder, the man took explicit photos that he shared with these women on Snapchat. What he didn't realize was that his photos and messages on his iPhone were synced up with an iCloud account he shared with his wife and his iPad-literate son.

His wife saw the pictures and messages, monitored the iCloud for more evidence and then divorced him on grounds of unreasonable behavior. She also was able to point out in the trial the emotional damage the couple's son could have suffered had he seen the inappropriate pictures and messages.[109]

LESSON: Practice caution when it comes to private photos. Be certain to check any syncing or sharing settings on your phone or other devices for your pictures or videos. Or, better still: don't cheat on your spouse.

• • • • •

Twitter helps during school shooting

During a school shooting at Lone Star College in Texas, students stuck inside the building were able to communicate with the outside world via Twitter. One student, Amanda, communicated a play by play of what she was experiencing including a tweet that read *"Everyone! There is a man shooting at Lonestar North Harris. This is not a joke. Please be safe. I'm so scared."* She was also able to contact a friend to tell her mother that she was safe. She was also contacted by CNN for more information and was sent well wishes from users located in Denmark.[110]

• • • • •

Don't text & drive!

After making the decision to text and drive, 20-something Jamie Nash lost control of her car before ultimately being pinned inside the car as it caught fire. She was trapped in her burning car for over 20 minutes. Nash, a mother, was fortunate her kids weren't in the car.

She suffered third and fourth degree burns over the majority of her body. She required 30 surgeries in two years to treat the burns. Feeling fortunate to survive her horrific accident, she became determined to spread the word to stop texting and driving. She tells her story at schools and businesses in hopes to educate people on the risks of texting and driving. According to the National Safety council, each year, 100,000 people crash while texting (U.S.). [111]

• • • • •

Don't text & walk!

Some studies show that texting and walking causes even more accidents than texting and driving and we know how bad that is. Dr. Dietrich Jehle, a professor of emergency medicine at the University of Buffalo in New York indicates that roughly 10% of all pedestrian emergencies involve a mobile device.[112]

An Ohio State study showed that ER visits tripled between 2004 to 2010 as a result of pedestrians texting while walking. Co-Study Author Dr. Jack L. Nasar, Ph.D., told *Heathline* that these "walking texters also pose a threat to innocent bystanders. It is more likely that they are going to walk into someone else and knock them over."[113]

Research out of Stony Brook[114] revealed that one is 61% more likely to veer off course when looking at their mobile device when walking than they are when not distracted.

If you can't stop texting, Jehle recommends:

1. Use the voice command ability of your phone

2. Pull out of the general flow of pedestrian traffic

3. Stop walking[115]

• • • • •

Wrestler stands tall and inspires on Facebook

"He's always done everything; he hasn't let anything hold him back. He doesn't want to be different," says Anthony Robles' mother. Only her son is different, he's an NCAA wrestling champion. Few people have earned this title, and fewer still have done it on one leg—Anthony Robles was born without a right leg.

"I had a dream of playing football growing up, but I was too small for that so I decided on wrestling," says Robles. "I was a terrible wrestler, only about 90 pounds, but my mom told me God made me for a reason, and I believe that reason [God made me] is for wrestling."

Robles didn't see his condition as an obstacle. In fact, he has used it to his benefit. "It is a great advantage; my grip is extremely strong from walking on crutches all day using my hands and shoulders. My upper body strength is a huge advantage in my weight class."

He even ran his first mile on crutches in ten minutes and then reduced his time to eight minutes. "I think he has a goal of doing it in six minutes on crutches and, knowing Anthony, he'll accomplish it," said an Arizona State teammate.

In 2011, Robles completed a perfect senior season by winning his final wrestling match 7-1. "I wrestle because I love wrestling, but it inspires me when I get kids, even adults, who write me on Facebook or send me letters in the mail saying that I've inspired them, and they look up to me, and they're motivated to do things that other people wouldn't have thought possible." [Source: *Digital Leader* by Erik Qualman]

LESSON: As a student, you can create a digital stamp that inspires others, just like Arizona State student athlete Anthony Robles. Just like Robles, your own unique hurdles are there for you to overcome and they will become part of your unique story and digital legacy.

· · · · ·

Welker's wife gone wild

After the AFC Championship game on January 20, 2013, Wes Welker's wife went on a Facebook rant after a frustrating loss. Anna Burns Welker posted a status that read,

"Proud of my husband and the Pats," Burns Welker wrote. "By the way, if anyone is bored, please go to Ray Lewis' Wikipedia page: 6 kids, 4 wives. Acquitted for murder. Paid a family off. Yay. What a hall of fame player! A true role model!"

She later apologized with a statement released to Larry Brown Sports. Burns Welker said, "I'm deeply sorry for my recent post on Facebook. I let the competitiveness of the game and the comments people were making about a team I dearly love get the best of me. My actions were emotional and irrational and I sincerely apologize to Ray Lewis and anyone affected by my comment after yesterday's game. It is such an accomplishment for any team to make it to the NFL playoffs, and the momentary frustration I felt should not overshadow the accomplishments of both of these amazing teams."[116]

LESSON: You represent your spouse, girlfriend, friends and family.

• • • • •

Bus driver saves child from fall becomes YouTube star

Steven St. Bernard, a New York City bus driver, was arriving home from work when he heard some commotion. A seven-year-old autistic child had climbed out of a nearby apartment window and was dancing on top of an air conditioning unit several stories up.

St. Bernard prayed that if the girl jumped he would get there in time. The girl did jump and St. Bernard made it just in time to catch her fall. The girl suffered no injuries. St. Bernard tore a tendon in his hand. This unbelievable event was captured on YouTube.

"He has a heart, a very good heart—kids, adults, anybody—he would do anything for anybody," neighbor, Jessica Aleman, said of St. Bernard.[117]

LESSON: Social media can capture beautifully heroic acts. Remember that the eye in the sky never lies.

Watch incredible video: http://bit.ly/IjNITG

• • • • •

Billionaire bullied

T. Boone Pickens, billionaire and oilman, and three of his children are suing his son Michael Pickens in Dallas County Court for alleged cyberbullying and cyberstalking. They are suing him for five counts: invasion of privacy, defamation, libel, harmful access by computer and extortion. In 2012, Michael started a blog called "5 Days in Connecticut."

In the blog, he discussed his drug addiction and recovery. He then began to talk about how his addiction was due to his father's abuse, the drug addiction of his siblings and other personal family matters.

He tweeted and emailed links of the blog to people within the business. News stations then obtained the tweets. According to court documents, Boone and his three children say that Michael is lying in hopes to extort $20 million from Boone.[118] The family is asking for damages at the maximum lawful rate.

LESSON: Bullying happens in families, business, everywhere...

· · · · ·

Twitter's ability to stop suicides

Health scientists at Brigham Young University have been researching the ability for Twitter to help prevent suicides by seeing warning signals. Their conclusion is that it can be an effective tool. The study indicates, "Twitter may be a viable tool for real-time monitoring of suicide risk factors on a large scale. Individuals who are at risk for suicide may be detected through social media."[119]

The researchers found that actually suicide rates mirror the rate of suicide chatter on Twitter, at the state level.

Health science professor at Brigham Young, Michael Barnes, believes, "The value of Twitter is that it is real time, and because it's real time, we have an opportunity to be taking action instead of looking at suicide data, suicide rates and saying 'What are we going to do?' If we can identify at-risk groups or populations, we're in a much better position to provide an intervention."[120]

LESSON: Social media, mobile and big data can be forces of good to prevent suicide.

· · · · ·

"And if you don't give a damn what people think, they just don't bother disapproving. That's genuinely been my experience. I was talking to a friend yesterday about the opinions of others, and this extraordinary social media thing about which I obviously know nothing...it seems that people are incredibly vulnerable to what people are saying about them in these...what do they call them, social networks. It's pretty serious; we've had a couple of girls commit suicide over it. It is incomprehensible to me that nybody would pay the slightest bit of attention to what somebody had said about them on a computer."[121]

Dervla Murphy, 50-year veteran travel author

· · · · ·

Twelve-year-old death the result of cyberbullying

Twelve-year-old Rebecca Sedwick leapt from atop a cement factory tower and plunged to her death. She was the victim of cyberbullying from 15 girls that ganged up on her online after she started dating a particular boy.

Sherriff Grady Judd was outraged stating, "I'm aggravated that the parents [of the bullies] aren't doing what parents should do. Responsible parents take disciplinary action. The parents do not think there is a problem here and that's a problem. One bullying suspect posted on Facebook: "Yes [I know] I bullied REBECCA and she killed herself but...I don't give a (expletive)."

Rebecca's mother sadly stated, "I can't say that I want these girls to spend the rest of their life in jail or any time in jail," she said, "but they do need serious rehabilitation."

LESSON: Parents need to take responsibility to ensure they set the right example for their kids and ensure they aren't bullies.

· · · · ·

Cyberbullying victim helps others fight online abuse

Paige Chandler, a cyberbullying victim, was attacked via Formspring. People would send her anonymous comments insulting her appearance calling her "ugly and fat."

At the age of 17, she also has joined CyberMentor.org.uk to help other victims of online abuse.[122]

LESSON: Anyone, old and young, can stand up and fight evil.

· · · · ·

Lessons Learned in Teams & Athletics

#ThanksCSU campaign creates digital space for alums posting it forward

A social media campaign is helping Cal State alumni thank the faculty and staff that positively influenced them. The #thankscsu campaign is part of Cal State's effort to reach three million alumni. They have created an online yearbook and graduates invited to thank a faculty or staff member who affected their lives and to post it to Facebook, Instagram or Twitter.[123]

LESSON: Create opportunities for alums of your team or organization to post it forward. Any hashtag or social media campaign that rallies your members or fellow teammates to share positive messages is a great way to build unity and a strong digital footprint for your organization.

• • • • •

#UglyGirlsClub fights hate with positivity online

When a student organization at Royal Holloway University in London overheard a rude male student calling them the "The Ugly Girls Club," they decided the best way to retaliate was to make light of the situation. The young women took to social media with tweets and pictures of themselves using the hashtag #uglygirlsclub. One tweet read, "Meet the #uglygirlsclub: student feminists sticking their tongue at the critics (literally!)" with a photo attached. The group changed their official Facebook page to #UglyGirlsClub and posted unflattering selfies to the page encouraging others to do the same. And they have. The Facebook page has over 5,000 members and is growing.[124]

LESSON: Turn lemons into digital lemonade. Your student team or organization can use social media platforms and mobile apps to start a movement greater than yourself.

· · · · ·

Snapchat used to recruit student athletes

New NCAA Division I recruiting rules allow coaches to use Snapchat as a way to recruit prospective players or share stories with their parents or guardians. Hernando Planells, assistant coach and recruiting coordinator for women's basketball at Duke University, finds Snapchat to be an excellent tool for recruiting new athletes as it allows the team to share a more behind the scenes view.

The team is using Snapchat to take pictures of practice or behind the scenes prepping for a game. Planells believes that the lack of formality on Snapchat allows for players to show their personality and the culture of the team.[125]

LESSON: Every team and organization has a culture. If it's a good culture, leverage it by showcasing the culture digitally. Students want to be a part of a strong culture. Use digital tools and mobile apps to share the "behind the scenes" look into your organization or team.

· · · · ·

Video helps man get recruited by Harlem Globetrotters

After posting a video onto YouTube, Jacob Tucker became famous. As an Illinois College basketball player, Tucker used the video of himself doing slam dunks as an audition for the college slam dunk championship contest. After winning an online fan vote on Facebook, he filled the final spot. The video was viewed over 3.1 million times. Tucker ended up winning the dunk contest and has since been recruited by the Harlem Globetrotters.

LESSON: One reason to use social media and mobile tools is so that the world can discover your talent.[126]

• • • • •

Kent State wrestler is indefinitely suspended due to insensitive tweets

Kent State University indefinitely suspended a student athlete from the University's wrestling team in February 2014 after a series of negative tweets using gay slurs. The target of the offensive tweets was former University of Missouri football player Michael Sam. The student and the University received an abundance of negative national attention for his posts. The University and the head wrestling coach issued public apologies for the student's behavior. After a series of other behavioral problems, the student was dismissed from the team, with the negative tweets being referenced in most articles about the student.[127]

LESSON: Response to poor digital decisions by a student athlete is not limited to just holding the individual accountable or losing playing time. The University was blitzed with negative publicity. This student's derogatory and homophobic tweets will follow him; forever.

• • • • •

PGA president gets impeached after inappropriate tweet

Professional Golf Association of America (PGA) President Ted Bishop was removed from his position one day following a series of insensitive and gender-based social media posts aimed at Ian Poulter, a European Golfer. The comments found on Bishop's Twitter and Facebook pages described Poulter as acting "...like a little school girl squealing during recess" and as a "Lil Girl." After attempting to apologize and resign, the PGA Board voted to impeach Bishop in spite of his apology.[128]

LESSON: When you represent an organization, you represent it 24 hours a day, especially on social media. Even in the spirit of competition, there is a level of accountability for organizational leaders for insensitive posts, which can result in loss of a job and no support from your employer at any level.

· · · · ·

Ohio State fan names his cancer Michigan. Beat Michigan.

Twelve-year-old Grant Reed from Ohio named his cancer "Michigan" in order to keep his spirits up after being diagnosed with brain cancer in 2011. He has beat Michigan and is currently in remission. After his story went nationwide, he has gotten a hospital visit from the Buckeyes' head coach Urban Meyer. He also got a call from Michigan head coach Brady Hoke inviting him and his family to the Ohio State-Michigan game. Grant's father, Troy, stated, "It's getting hard to keep my dislike for them, because they've been so classy and unbelievable to us."[129]

LESSON: Sometimes the person that seems like the enemy in a story can actually be the hero. Do not make assumptions.

· · · · ·

Roddy White's emotional tweets get the better of him

After George Zimmerman was found not guilty for the death of Trayvon Martin, Atlanta Falcons receiver Roddy White went to twitter to react to the verdict. Many athletes took to Twitter to voice their opinions, but White's took a turn for the worst.

He tweeted, "All them jurors should go home tonight and kill themselves for letting a grown man get away with killing a kid."

That Sunday, he tweeted an apology saying, "I understand my tweet last nite [sic] was extreme. I never meant for the people to do that. I was shocked and upset about the verdict. I am sorry."[130]

LESSON: Measure your words twice and post once, especially when it involves an emotional topic.

• • • • •

Tweet costs student athlete his scholarship

In July of 2014, Penn State University Assistant Football Coach, Herb Hand, made the decision not to offer a scholarship to a potential football recruit based on their social media activity. "If a guy makes the decision to post or RT stuff that degrades women, references drug use or cyber-bullying crap, then I can make the decision to drop them... Especially if I have discussed it with them prior, and especially in today's climate of athletics," said Hand. [131]

LESSON: This example warns student-athletes that coaches are paying attention to social media, and that poor digital behavior can outweigh high performance on the field. The next time an athlete goes online, they should ask themselves, could tweeting, retweeting, or liking an offensive post cost you a scholarship?

• • • • •

Even 310-pound football players can be bullied

Jonathan Martin was a starting player for the Miami Dolphins when he suddenly left the team. His lawyer indicated his reason for departure was the result of bullying from his teammates and one teammate in particular, Richie Incognito.

There is much we can learn from this story. What's interesting is this incident involving two grown men (both over 300 pounds) exhibits some of the standard traits of teenage bullying.

1. Victim is blamed; many blamed Martin for not standing up for himself.

2. Poor advice and leadership from people that should know better (the General Manager told Martin's agent that Martin should just simply punch Incognito in the face).[132]

LESSON: Bullying and hazing occurs beyond the middle school playground. If it can happen in the National Football League, then it can happen in your business or organization.

• • • • •

Lessons Learned in Crime & Politics

UK man jailed for sarcastic threats against airport

Paul Chambers, a UK based tax accountant, was planning to fly out of Robin Airport. To his disappointment, he discovered the airport was closed and his flight cancelled. An avid Twitter user, Chambers immediately posted:

> "Robin Hood airport is closed. You've got a week and a bit to get your **** together otherwise I'm blowing the airport sky high!"

While Chambers later indicated he was satirically messing around, a Robin Airport employee didn't find it such a laughing matter. He immediately alerted the authorities about Chambers' post. Chambers was apprehended by police at his office, was convicted and fined 385 British Pounds for a post deemed "menacing" in its content. Chambers also lost his job.[133]

LESSON: Joking about terrorist attacks either offline or online is no laughing matter and can have serious consequences.

• • • • •

Digital deputies

Looters and rioters in Vancouver following Game 7 of the 2011 Stanley Cup Finals learned a tough lesson. Photos and video posted online helped police conduct "Facebook justice" and arrest hundreds of violators. Many of these citizens not only received criminal punishment, but also subsequently lost their jobs. Unlike in the offline world where there may only be a handful of eyewitnesses, online there are millions of digital deputies.[134]

• • • • •

Silk Road shutdown:
Site that sold heroin & hit men shutdown

Silk Road, a nefarious site that sold everything from heroin to murder, was eventually discovered and shut down. FBI agent Christopher Tarbell said, "The site succeeded to make conducting illegal transactions on the Internet as easy and frictionless as shopping online at mainstream e-commerce websites."[135]

Founder, Ross Ulbricht, 29, used a complex system underground network "onion router" or "thor" to bounce encrypted message across various machines globally. This makes it incredibly difficult to track the origin of messages and transactions. As a result, Silk Road was able to develop a billion dollar business.

Authorities eventually caught Ulbricht when he posted, using his own name, a question on a public message board seeking assistance for a complex coding issue around Silk Road.

LESSON: No matter how technically savvy you are at hiding things...there is always someone better at uncovering them.

● ● ● ● ●

Texting teen sentenced for 15 years

A Massachusetts teenager was condemned to prison and lost his license for 15 years for causing a fatal crash. His mobile data usage showed he was texting when the accident occurred. This was used in the court of law to help convict him.[136]

LESSON: Texting and driving kills. Your mobile data can and will be used in a court of law.

● ● ● ● ●

What's on your phone can and will be used against you

Boston police arrested Brima Wurie on a minor charge and confiscated his phone. They then noticed an unusual amount of calls coming in from a known drug house and as a result were able to book him later on drug dealing.

San Diego police pulled over David Riley for having expired tags. Pictures on Riley's phone incriminated Riley as being part of a gang shooting in 2009.

LESSON: There is an ongoing legal debate about privacy (Fourth Amendment), mobile devices and their use in the legal system, but mobile phones and what's on them can often be used against you in the court of law.[137]

· · · · ·

Confessing drunk driving manslaughter on YouTube

Matthew Cordle admitted in a YouTube video that he was responsible for killing a man via drinking and driving. In it, Cordle explains, "This video will act as my confession. When I get charged, I will plead guilty and take full responsibility for everything I've done to Vincent and his family. I won't dishonor Vincent's memory by lying about what happened." Cordle dismissed attorney's advice to lie and that his Breathalyzer test could be thrown out of court. "All I would have to do is lie," Cordle stated, "I won't go down that path." [138]

LESSON: The world is radically different than it was a decade ago.

· · · · ·

Losing a presidency

While running for president, Mitt Romney discovered how nothing is confidential. Romney made some ill-advised comments at a private fundraising event. What Romney failed to realize is he was being secretly video recorded. His famous "47% line" went like this:

> *"All right, there are 47% who are with him (President Obama), who are dependent upon government, who believe that they are victims, who believe the government has a responsibility to care for them ... And they will vote for this president no matter what ... These are people who pay no income tax ... My job is not to worry about those people. I'll never convince them they should take personal responsibility and care for their lives."*[39]

LESSON: Video can now act as evidence in the court systems which may or may not benefit those in trial.

· · · · ·

Hit & post

18-year-old Jacob Cox-Brown was arrested by Astoria (Oregon) police nine hours after posting "Drivin drunk ... classsic ;) but to whoever's vehicle i hit i am sorry. :P"[40]

Two people digitally connected Cox-Brown's sent messages to the Astoria police alerting them. This clue was vital in the police linking Cox-Brown to a 1 a.m. hit and run involving two other parked vehicles. Without the post, the police most likely would not have solved this particular hit-and-run incident.

· · · · ·

Naked profile pictures exposed

Floridian Joseph Bernard Campbell was charged with hacking into 19 different women's Facebook accounts and stealing nude or semi-nude photos of the women. He then later hacked into these women's accounts and posted these pilfered photos as their main profile picture.

Many of the victims found out from friends calling them and asking, "Did you know what's on your Facebook page?"

Campbell indicated that he knew most of the women and his intent was "to harass the victims and cause them emotional distress."[141]

Many of the photos that Campbell stole were private photos sent from women, via Facebook, to their fiancés serving overseas in the military.

Campbell pleaded guilty to charges of cyber-stalking and unauthorized access to a computer. Each of these crimes has a maximum penalty of five years in federal prison along with a $250,000 fine.

• • • • •

Murder for hire

London Eley digitally posted about her ex-boyfriend and father of her child, Corey White, "I will pay somebody a stack to kill my baby father." "Baby father" is in reference to White and a "stack" is slang for $1,000.

Timothy Bynum responded with, "Say no more ... what he look like ... where he be at ... need that stack 1st. [sic]"

Eley and Bynum were arrested and charged with solicitation to commit murder, terroristic threat charges and attempted murder.

White was killed a few months later. Authorities weren't certain if the posts were linked to his death.[142]

• • • • •

• • • • •

*The greatness of a man is not in
how much wealth he acquires, but in his
integrity and his ability to affect
those around him positively.*

BOB MARLEY

• • • • •

CHAPTER

3

NOTE: Digital resources listed
are free for users unless
noted otherwise.

TOP 15 DIGITAL REPUTATION TOOLS

No. **1**

Brand Yourself

Brand Yourself puts the power of reputation management in your own hands by providing tools for a do-it-yourself digital reputation audit. Users can actively improve their own Google results. Key features include the ability for users to submit links they would like to appear when someone searches their name on Google, the ability to track your progress via emailed custom alerts, and the ability to send notifications when your name is Googled.

brandyourself.com

No. **2**

Buffer

Buffer is a free tool that shares your content across the web at the best possible times throughout the day so that your followers and fans see your updates more frequently.

bufferapp.com

Buzz Bundle

Buzz Bundle is a service that provides social media management tools to handle all your social media and reputation management activities. Companies and individuals can use Buzz Bundle for posting, responding and joining conversations on a variety of social media outlets. (Cost: $199)

buzzbundle.com

Epic Browser

Epic Browser is a web browser that aims to improve user privacy by defaulting to private browsing mode thus preventing the recording of history, caches, passwords and other features that may reveal information about the user. Key features include private browsing as well as the ability to clear all browsing data automatically once your session is complete.

epicbrowser.com

Google Alerts

Google Alerts are email updates of the latest relevant Google results (web, news, etc.) based on your queries. You may choose to set up a Google Alert for your name, business or organization as a way to monitor your digital reputation. You can control the number and frequency of the alerts as well as the email address to which the alerts are connected. Most of us should use this to track our name and the name of our organization.

google.com/alerts

Google Analytics

Google Analytics is a tool offered by Google that not only provides extensive data about a website's traffic and traffic sources but also measures conversions and sales. When monitoring your digital reputation, Google Analytics can provide vital information about web traffic that will help you become more strategic. It can also tell you the demographics of people who visit your pages.

google.com/analytics

Hootsuite

Hootsuite is a free tool that allows you to monitor activity on all social networks easily. You may choose to monitor all tweets that include your name or the name of your company, product or organization. Hootsuite pulls all keywords that you want tracked into one easy to read column. Popular features include the ability to post one message to all your social networks simultaneously, an ability to store your favorite posts, and the opportunity to pre-schedule social media posts.

hootsuite.com/features/mobile-apps/iphone

Kindr

Kindr is an iPhone app that makes it fun and easy to brighten someone's day by sending short, thoughtful, and often funny, messages. Post it forward with ease!

kindr.me/

Klout

Klout is a website and mobile app designed to measure online social influence using an algorithm that analyzes a user's social media platforms in terms of size and engagement. A Klout score is one way that you, or your brand can reach across platforms and measure key reputation components including influence. Popular features include the Klout score, an ability to score your digital influence as well as a list of topics, which describe your influence within your network. The scores range from 0-100, with 100 the best.

Movie producers often use Klout when they launch a movie premiere in a new city. For example, if a new movie, starring Selma Hayek, is set to premiere in Miami than the producers would have Klout send a message to all Miami area users who have a Klout score of 80 or above in terms of movie influence. The user would receive an invitation to attend the movie premiere and meet Selma Hayek. The guests would arrive, enjoy their premiere experience and post items to their digital followers.

During Fashion Week in New York, some of the exclusive parties only allowed access to individuals who possessed a Klout score of 70 or higher.

klout.com/home

Kred

Similar to Klout, Kred is a tool designed to measure influence. Kred is unique because it is the first and only influence measuring tool to publicly share the algorithm they use to identify a user's score. Kred can help you or your brand measure influence within a specific community of interest. Popular features include the ability to view leading influencers within a specific digital community, a transparent process and algorithm for measuring influence, and a detailed monthly reporting of engagement and outreach.

kred.com

LinkedIn

LinkedIn is the number one social platform for developing a professional network, finding new job opportunities and building a digital reputation. Users should complete their profile in its entirety. The reason? According to LinkedIn, a complete LinkedIn profile receives 40 times more opportunities than an incomplete profile. Key features of LinkedIn include: the ability to connect with professionals...ability to create a detailed searchable professional profile, and excellent job boards.

linkedin.com/

Namecheap for Education

If you're interested in kickstarting your online presence, and you are a student then this is a great resource. The Namecheap Student Bundle includes a free .ME domain (one year), free about.me Premium or GitHub Page, and a free private email account.

nc.me

Reputation Alert (iOS)

Reputation Alert is an iOS mobile app that monitors keywords on Twitter. Users can set names, brands, organizations or specific product names as keywords and monitor any Twitter mentions. (Cost: $0.99)

apple.com/1BYVYMv

Socialmention.com

Socialmention.com is a search tool specifically designed to search social networking sites. This tool monitors one's presence across various social media platforms. Popular features include filterable results, sentiment analysis reporting, listing of top hashtags, as well as users associated with each search query.

socialmention.com

WhosTalkin

WhosTalkin is branded as a blog search tool. This sophisticated tool allows users to search for conversations surrounding topics they most value. The site has a simple design that allows the user to search across blogs, major news sites, social media networks and much more. It provides brands and individuals with comprehensive reporting of keyword mentions in order to monitor reputation effectively.

whostalkin.com

• • • • •

"I would rather go to any extreme than suffer anything that is unworthy of my reputation, or of that of my crown."

ELIZABETH I

• • • • •

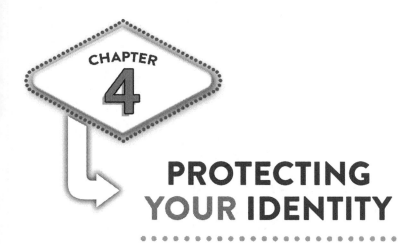

PROTECTING YOUR IDENTITY

Identity theft is the fastest growing crime in the United States.[143] Criminals use information from our social networks to poach our identity. Below are 20 tips to help prevent you from becoming a victim.

20 Tactical Tips to Protect Your Identity

Be careful with under the door menus

Whether you are in a hotel or your own home, be wary of menus slipped under your door. Identity thieves often use these fake menus to capture your personal and credit card information when you call the restaurant. To assure your safety, go online or contact the hotel's front desk to place an order.

Your Smartphone is vulnerable

Make sure your computers, mobile devices and wearable technology have the latest security software. Neglecting to frequently update this software can put the information stored in your devices at risk.

_No._ 3

Do not use public Wi-Fi for financial transactions

If you are using public Wi-Fi in a hotel or restaurant, do not go online for banking, stock trades or other important financial matters. Perform these transactions in the safety of your home. Similarly, do not use publicly shared computers for such transactions. For example, if you are in the library, do not access your investment account. Identity thieves have "keylogging" software on these machines, which track everything you push on the keyboard.

_No._ 4

Beware of free Wi-Fi

Identify thieves often name Wi-Fi hotspots as official connections for various locations, including hotels, airports or restaurants. For example, the hotspot might be named "freewifi" or "hotelwifi." If you use these unsecured networks, you are at risk. If you are uncertain which is the correct Wi-Fi, simply ask an airport official, desk clerk or waitress.

_No._ 5

Avoid phishing scams

Should you receive solicitations from companies, banks or other organizations, do not click on the links. It is much safer to go directly to the home pages of these sites to find the specific offer or issue. If you choose to click through, make certain that the URL is correct. Example: _www.bankofamerica.com_ not *bankofamerica.randomsite.com.* Phishers develop fake company web pages and fake company emails presenting themselves as reputable companies. The phishers are now in position to steal your password and personal information.

Be very suspicious of requests for your personal information from anyone including your email provider. Triple-check to ensure the request is legitimate before taking any action. Your email provider will rarely send you a message, so be alert when you receive one and make sure it is not a phishing scam.

≡ (*No.* 6) ≡

Set up a password for online card use

Do not post important personal information on social networks. Choose personal security questions that cannot be answered by your Facebook information.

≡ (*No.* 7) ≡

Be careful on online auctions, such as eBay

Pay the seller directly with a credit card so you can dispute the charges if the merchandise does not arrive or is misrepresented. Whenever possible, avoid paying by check or money order.

≡ (*No.* 8) ≡

Destroy digital data

When you sell, trade or dispose of a computer system, a hard drive, a recordable CD, backup tape or DVD, you must take precautions to ensure the data is completely and irrevocably destroyed. Deleting the data or reformatting the hard drive is insufficient. Anyone with technological savviness can undelete files or recover data from a formatted drive. Use a product like ShredXP to ensure that data on hard drives is completely destroyed. Physically destroy CD, DVD or tape media by breaking or shattering before disposal or use shredders that are specifically designed for this purpose.

No. 9

Use strong passwords for all online accounts

Use a strong password that includes symbols, numbers and upper and lower case letters to protect your identity. If you have a hard time making up a strong password, try using a mnemonic device. For example, "I was born at New York Mercy Hospital in 1975" becomes "Iwb@NYMHi1975." Vary your passwords because thieves have easier access to your personal information when you use the same password for each account.

No. 10

Limit the personal information you share online

The number of available social networks increases daily and your personal information is available to anyone. Protect yourself from identity thieves by not posting personal information, especially your address, phone numbers, SSN, birth date or birthplace.

No. 11

Be careful when shopping online

Use secure sites when shopping online and research unfamiliar sites to ensure they are real. When checking the security of the website, look for https://. The "s" that is displayed after "http" indicates the website is secure. The "s" is occasionally invisible until you move to the order page. Thieves use shopping websites to collect credit card numbers and other private information.

$$\equiv \left(\text{No.} \atop 12\right) \equiv$$

Confirmation of order

Once your online purchase is complete, you will receive a confirmation page that summarizes your order and includes your customer information, product information and confirmation number. Screen shot one copy of the confirmation page as well as the page delineating company name, postal address, phone number and legal terms, including return policy. Keep these for your own records for the period covered by the return/warranty policy. The merchant may also email a confirmation message. Screen shot that message as well as any other company correspondence.

$$\equiv \left(\text{No.} \atop 13\right) \equiv$$

Keep track of personal information

Do not carry your extra credit cards, social security card, birth certificate or passport in your wallet or purse unless absolutely necessary. This practice minimizes the information a thief can steal.

$$\equiv \left(\text{No.} \atop 14\right) \equiv$$

Check your credit report

Order a copy of your credit report periodically to ensure your information is accurate and includes only those activities you authorized. When you require credit to buy a home or obtain a credit card, unresolved issues will not stand in the way of a successful outcome.

No. 15

Destroy hotel key cards

Hotel magnetic key cards contain all the personal information you provided to the front desk staff. Cut the cards in half and destroy them.

No. 16

Ask for credit card verification

Your signature on the back of your credit card validates the card and expresses agreement with the banks' terms. When you place "SEE ID" on the card, you inform the clerks to check the name and signature on the card against a driver's license.

No. 17

Sign out

Website logins have added a "stay signed in" or "keep me signed in" check box. Do not use this option! *Always* uncheck this box, especially when using a shared computer. This option appears convenient, but checking "stay signed in" to your account allows hackers to access your personal information easily.

No. 18

Be aware of your surroundings

Criminals can access your personal information quickly and easily, through their camera phones. Therefore, be wary of people standing extremely close to you when you are using your debit or credit card. Make every effort to use the same ATM so you can tell when the equipment looks different. When entering your PIN number in an ATM, position your body so others cannot see the keys you are pressing.

Close all unused credit card accounts and bank accounts.

No. 19

Keep copies of cards and documents

Keep copies of all your identification cards, credit cards and other important documents. You now have the 1-800 phone numbers and account numbers to contact the credit card company in the event your card is lost or stolen.

No. 20

Treat mail with care

Always deposit outgoing mail containing personally identifying information in a post office collection box or at the post office rather than an unsecured mailbox and collect your mail daily. Consider a switch to paperless billing by contacting your bank, credit card provider or other companies from whom you receive mailed bills. Contact the United States Postal Service to request a vacation hold if you plan to be away from home and no one is available to pick up your mail. The United States Postal Service will hold your mail at your local post office for a select period of time until you can pick it up.

SOCIAL MEDIA AND YOUR CAREER

Tips for showcasing your work online, leveraging your digital presence to land your dream job, and using social media to build your network.

LinkedIn Success Tips for Students

Research shows that 93% of human resources officers use information found online to evaluate candidates most or all of the time.[144] With this statistic in mind, students should first visit their Career Service offices or faculty who are experts in the field of interest when preparing to secure an internship. These resources can be great tools to help prepare for the internship application process. For example, faculty and career service staff can teach students about the type of online profile that employers who offer internships are seeking. Using this information to create or refine digital identity can be a great way to help show that a student is a highly desirable candidate. A few tips for students include:

No.
1

Create an account on LinkedIn with your real name that highlights academic major, leadership activities, community service, research with faculty, and current and past employment. Capture all helpful tips from faculty and career services officers to make your page as robust as possible.

No.
2

Take time to secure a professional photo for your account. Be certain to use this photo for other social media accounts, even if they are private. Many times employers can find your other accounts through Google, and even if the posts are hidden, the main image should be consistent with your public presence. Be sure to avoid any pictures that are not congruent with your professional image.

No.
3

Be consistent in posting articles or links that are related to your aspirational career. Employers will want to see that you are keeping up with current events in the industry, and this can even help them shape questions for your interview. Be sure that your posts are relatively low on opinions and more focused on content and facts.

Joining LinkedIn groups related to your career aspirations and following organizations and companies related to the field can also be helpful. Make sure that information you post is relevant and furthers the discussion in groups, and isn't posted just for the sake of posting.

If groups have chats or active times to engage noted professionals in the field, be certain to participate actively by asking thoughtful questions and sharing pertinent information. If you have a public Facebook or Twitter page that is used professionally, there are similar opportunities to actively use social media for branding and marketing.

· · · · ·

"The task of the modern educator is not to cut down jungles, but to irrigate deserts."

C. S. LEWIS

· · · · ·

5 Portfolio Websites You Can Use to Showcase Your Skills

Clippings.me

Specifically designed to help writers organize their work, Clippings.me allows users to customize pages and post clips by link or uploading a document. There are free and premium options with varied levels of customization based on what you are willing to pay. As a student, you do a lot of writing, and more and more employers are looking for writing samples. Having your writing samples all in one place easily sharable with employers will set you apart from other candidates.

clippings.me

LiveBinders

Forget the old ways of lugging in your binder to every interview filled with papers, examples of your work, and any other portfolio items. LiveBinders lets you combine uploaded documents, links, and multimedia content into a simple online package that is perfect for sharing. Also, you can add your own description to each item so an employer can peruse your work without you being there to explain it live.

livebinders.com

Behance

Behance removes the barriers between talent and opportunity. The portfolio site is perfect for graphic or web designers looking to showcase their work. Behance has a great community and companies explore work and access talent on a global scale. It is an excellent place for those majoring in any creative field to begin building their network before they need it!

behance.net

Google Sites

While it has more of a "plain" look, Google Sites can be great alternatives to a more labor intensive personal portfolio site. They are easy to set up and can easily showcase any Google docs, YouTube videos or links to other examples of your work.

sites.google.com

Journo Portfolio

Are you a journalism or communications major? This is a great site to showcase all your work and build a network within your industry. Journo Portfolio is a site specifically designed for writing portfolios. Your profile lists how many publications you've written for, how many pieces you've written, as well as when your page was last updated. Users can really make their sites attractive using the sleek layouts provided and user-friendly interface. As with many sites, if you want controls beyond the basic, there is a small monthly cost.

journoportfolio.com

• • • • •

"Think about what people are doing on Facebook today. They're keeping up with their friends and family, but they're also building an image and identity for themselves, which in a sense is their brand. They're connecting with the audience that they want to connect to. It's almost a disadvantage if you're not on it now."

MARK ZUCKERBERG

• • • • •

CHAPTER 6

CYBERBULLYING, ONLINE HARASSMENT AND SEXUAL VIOLENCE

Some of these items are review from our opening rules section, but this is such an important topic that it bears repeating. Research shows that 40% of Internet users report being harassed online, and over 50% say that they do not know the harasser. With 63% of people reporting that the Internet allows for more anonymity in their online life than their offline life, this is one of the key factors resulting in online harassment.[145]

However, if you are reading this book, you know that what you post online is not necessarily anonymous. Just because one is typing a nasty or demeaning comment in the privacy of their home doesn't mean their 600 followers won't see it on Twitter. The highest levels of harassment were reported by those under the age of 35, meaning that if we don't begin to do something about this, the problem will only continue to grow.[146]

In this section, you can read about other young people that have experienced online harassment, what is currently being done by organizations, universities and companies to help prevent online harassment, and tips for students that are dealing with online harassment.

Bystander VS. Upstander

Bystander: one who is present but not taking part in the situation or event

Upstander: one who is willing to stand up and take action in defense of others [147]

We encourage all students to serve as upstanders when they witness any cyberbullying or online harassment. The following section includes tips for students that are experiencing some form of online harassment, as well as tips for students that want to be upstanders and help end cyberbullying and online harassment.

Hazing

Hazing is never appropriate, be it on an athletic team, in a fraternity or sorority, or in any organization. Hazing involves forcing someone to perform strenuous, often humiliating and sometimes dangerous actions on others as a part of an initiation or ritual. College campuses have strict rules against hazing and it is also illegal. If you are being hazed, tell someone. If you are participating in hazing someone, stop.

Social media often brings secrets to light and the consequences are amplified. It can also be used as a means for you to uncover hazing in a potential organization of which you hope to be a part. Do research on any group you hope to join. If you see something that is not right, tell someone.

Hazing can also occur online and often involves bullying. If you are being hazed online, follow the suggestions listed in this book under bullying.

Sexual Violence

Cyberbullying, stalking, and other forms of behavior online can contribute to and facilitate the continuation of sexual violence. Sexual violence online may include, but is not limited to a number of different acts:

- Sending unsolicited texts of a sexual nature (sexts)
- Communications that threaten sexual assault
- The continuation of domestic abuse and abusive relationship patterns online
- The tracking of an individual's movements and actions
- Luring individuals into sexual situations or soliciting individuals for sex
- The recording and dissemination of sexual acts without consent

These acts can occur regardless of an individual's gender identity or expression and are often a combination of offline and online actions.

Research indicates these acts occur far too often. A 2014 report found that **young adults**, those 18-29, are more likely than any other demographic group to experience online harassment. Thirteen percent of men ages 18-24 are experiencing sexual harassment online, and 25% of women were in the same age range as their target of online sexual harassment. In addition, college-aged women are receiving physical threats and sustained harassment offline at heightened rates.[148] Roughly 73% of sexual assaults involve someone the survivor (victim) knows.[149]

"One in five women are sexually assaulted in college. Most often, it's by someone she knows—and also most often, she does not report what happened. Many survivors are left feeling isolated, ashamed or to blame. Although it happens less often, men, too, are victims of these crimes."
—White House Sexual Assault Task Force[150]

If you are a victim of sexual violence, there is no one "right" way to handle it.

There are multiple options for next steps that you can explore both online and offline. Your school may offer offices that provide help that is specialized for victims of sexual violence. Other options you may want to consider are campus support staff members and student paraprofessionals like your resident assistant (RA), a University staff member or advisor, or the police. Digital resources can also serve as a great first step as many of them provide online communities for survivors, anonymous hotlines and forums, as well as digital communities for survivors. Below is a list of 5 digital resources we recommend.

5 Digital Resources for Victims of Sexual Violence

The Online Hotline

This is a 24/7 service that provides live, secure, anonymous crisis support for victims of sexual violence, their friends, and families over RAINN's website. RAINN is a national organization and it stands for Rape Abuse & Incest National Network. The Online Hotline is free of charge.

rainn.org/get-help/national-sexual-assault-online-hotline

Pandora's Project: Victim Message Boards and Forum

Pandora's Project welcomes all survivors of sexual violence, and offers a message board and chat room, free lending library, and numerous articles and resources for victims. Their online support group is free to join and is safely moderated by a diverse group of survivors.

pandys.org

End Rape On Campus (EROC) Website

EROC is a digital resource for victims of sexual violence on campus, as well as an excellent learning tool for students interested in helping to end rape on campus. If a victim feels that their institution did not handle their case properly through the student conduct process, EROC provides guidance as well as an EROC staff member to help victims file a federal complaint against the institution.

endrapeoncampus.org

National Sexual Violence Resource Center (NSVRC)

The NSVRC website provides a wide range of resources on sexual violence including statistics, research, position statements, statutes, training curricula, prevention initiatives and program information. This is a great online resource for victims and for students that want to educate their peers about sexual violence.

nsvrc.org

Not Alone

Information for students, schools, and anyone interested in finding resources on how to respond to and prevent sexual assault on college and university campuses and in our schools.

notalone.gov

It's On Us

It's On Us is a U.S. federally funded awareness campaign to help put an end to sexual assault on college campuses across the United States. The purpose of this campaign is for men and women across America "to make a personal commitment to step off the sidelines and be part of the solution to campus sexual assault."[151] The hope for this campaign is to shift the way people think about sexual assault and to inspire everyone that they can do something, big or small, to prevent sexual violence.

The Office of the President is urging students to sign the pledge to speak out and help keep their friends safe from sexual assault.[152] *It's On Us* has gained many partners such as: Electronic Arts (EA), Viacom, NCAA, Big Ten Conference, Big Twelve Conference, Microsoft-Bing, Tumblr and many more.[153]

Students and faculty from Boston University, University of Louisville, Eastern Illinois University, Clemson University, Michigan State University along with many more have created videos stating facts about sexual assault and how it is their responsibility to stop it.[154]

Other schools including New York University, George Washington University, Bridgewater College, Vanderbilt University and many more are having their students sign the pledge and spread the word about *It's On Us*. Getting more students involved leads to more awareness and more prevention. You can get involved today, yes even if you are outside the United States – this is a global epidemic.

itsonus.org.

Does your campus have these types of sexual assault policies (below chart) in place?

Individual	Peer/Partner	Organization	Community
Build bystander intervention and healthy relationship skills and establish positive norms about gender, sexuality and violence with evidence-informed interactive, multi-session intervention for incoming students	• Coach-implemented intervention for male athletes addressing hyper-masculine peer norms that support or facilitate sexual violence • Dorm-based intervention that reinforces positive norms and skills related to bystander behavior and healthy sexuality	• Engage campus leadership to promote culture of safety and respect • Social marketing campaign to addess norms related to sexual violence • Hot spot mapping to identify and monitor unsafe areas on campus	• Community initiatives to implement/enforce alcohol policy efforts to reduce excessive alcohol use or problem outlets • Strengthen/support enforcement, response, and reporting policies on- and off-campus

Consistent Message Across Campus Policies and Programs

The above chart was developed by the Centers for Disease Control and Prevention for use by the White House Task Force to Protect Students from Sexual Assault [Division of Violence Prevention, Centers for Disease Control and Prevention, Sarah DeGue, Ph.D.][155]

Tips for Students

When you're posting online:

- Think about how the receiver may interpret your messages. How would you feel if someone posted this about you?
- Remember that it is easy to be misunderstood online when you do not have the benefit of seeing someone's body language or hearing their tone.
- Sometimes it's better to talk to someone offline.

Sometimes it's difficult to tell when your own behavior crosses a line. Some things to consider:

- Avoid posting content that others may find offensive. Remember who your audience is.

There are also some steps you can take to secure your account.

- Log off all online accounts, especially accounts on public computers.
- Set your privacy settings.
- Do not share your password.

There are some resources that can help you if you are a victim or if you try to navigate these conversations. Read your campus' student code of conduct. Know your campus' computer use policies since you are subject to them if you use campus internet. Your college and university may also have rules and regulations regarding social media use. Be sure to review these rules if you're not already familiar with them.

Preventing Cyberbullying and Online Harassment

14 Ways to Prevent and Stop Cyberbullying

1. Do not communicate with cyberbullies.

2. Notify the abuser's online service.

3. Search online to ensure there are no photos or compromising personal information, which could be used against you.

4. Think twice before posting anything that could hurt someone's reputation.

5. Do not put anything online that other people might find offensive.

6. Encourage your children to seek help from an adult whenever they feel threatened.

7. Never share your password.

8. Log off all online accounts, especially accounts on public computers.

9. Set your privacy settings.

10. If you witness bullying, tell the offender to stop; hurtful behavior is unacceptable.

11. Activities that are illegal offline are often illegal online.

12. When you witness bullying and choose to ignore that behavior, your silence implies acceptance. Be an "upstander," not a bystander.

13. Do not send messages when you are angry.

14. Do not be a cyberbully. Model appropriate behavior.

Tips for Student Victims of Online Harassment and Cyberbullying

You may feel shame or even embarrassed to tell someone that you are a victim of these types of assaults. Do not be. Your best option is to tell someone. Take advantage of your university's or college's resources.

If you are a victim, here are some tips that can help you resolve the issue.

1. Remember that you are not deserving of this and you do not need to take it.

2. Tell that individual to stop. Send a clear brief message that states, "Please stop contacting me. I do not want to communicate with you anymore."

3. Keep screenshots, records, and save the bullying, harassing, or stalking messages. If you wish to take action against the individual(s) in the future, you will need to provide evidence.

4. Stop communicating with that individual. Don't respond to any of their attempts to interact with you. If the social media platform you are using allows you to block that person, block them.

5. Tell a university staff member. If you live on campus, tell your resident assistant or your resident director. You can also reach out to campus police or any other university official. There are a number of options available to you if you are being harassed or stalked. A staff member can help walk you through your options. These options can range from an inter-university barring of contact or a student conduct case to criminal proceedings. You have control in this process.

Reporting CyberBullying and Online Harassment on Popular Social Media Applications

The following section outlines the protocol for reporting online harassment on 5 of the most popular social media networks. If you are being harassed on a site or mobile application not listed below, we have found that most sites will have more information in their help section and encourage you to check there first.

Instagram

Instagram is a platform where students can share personal photos, videos, and tag their location.

If you or someone you know is being bullied through an Instagram photo, that photo can be reported via the following form:

Report Harassment or Bullying on Instagram

Fill out this form to report photos, videos, comments or profiles on Instagram that are bullying or harassing others. Please provide as many details as possible to help us review this issue.

Do you have an Instagram account?

○ Yes
○ No

Are you blocked from viewing the content you're trying to report?

○ Yes
○ No

Where is this happening?

Choose one:

○ In a photo
○ In a video
○ In comments on a photo or video
○ An entire profile is abusive

Are you able to access the content you want to report?

○ Yes
○ No

Learn how to get a link to a photo or video on Instagram.

Link to the photo you're reporting:

Description of the photo and why it's abusive:

What country are you reporting from?

Enter a country name...

Send

Photo Credit: *Instagram. (Producer). (January 19 2013) [logo]*

By providing a link to the offending photo and explaining why it is abusive, Instagram will check on the photo and take the necessary actions to resolve the issue.

If bullying is happening through a comment on an Instagram photo, the comment can be reported through the same form. On that same form, indicate that you are reporting a comment by selecting the comment option, and provide the link to the exact comment. Finally provide a description of why it is abusive. If you do not have access to the photo or comment, Instagram asks you have a friend copy and send the URL so you can report it. Instagram does not only encourage users to report bullying but they also offer support and advice for those affected by it.

Twitter

To report bullying or abusive behavior on Twitter, the site provides the following form. You can use the form to report something that is offensive to you or to someone you know. You'll need to identify the username that is sending the offensive or abusive tweets and provide a classification of the type of harassment you are experiencing using the categories they provide on the form.

Photo Credit: *support.twitter.com/forms/abusiveuser*

Facebook

If a Facebook post is abusive towards you or a friend, Facebook makes it easy to report in just one step. All of the following sources can be considered when reporting abuse: your profile, someone else's profile, photos, messages, and comments. Below is a visual of how you can report a post as abusive or harassment.

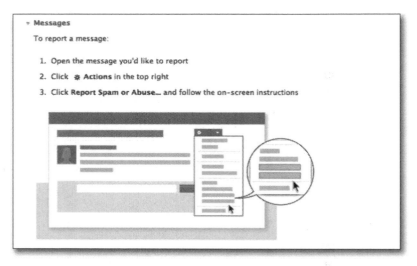

Photo Credit: *www.facebook.com/help/181495968648557*

· · · · ·

"I realized that bullying never has to do with you. It's the bully who's insecure."

SHAY MITCHELL

· · · · ·

Snapchat

SnapChat encourage users to report snaps that are a form of harassment through the web-based version of their app. You must access the site on a desktop in order to report abuse or harassment. To do so, go to the support page on Snapchat.com and fill out the following form indicating your information, the information of the online abuser and explain what you are reporting and why it is considered abusive.

Report Harassment

We take abuse and safety issues very seriously and we appreciate your taking the time to report an incident.

Please review our Community Guidelines and fill out any applicable parts of the form below to the best of your ability.

Be sure to include the Snapchat usernames of any accounts involved and some details about what happened.

> What's your Snapchat username?

> email address

I am reporting a:

> Select an option ⬍

> Recipient's username

How old is the recipient?

> Select an option ⬍

> Sender's username

How old is the sender?

> Select an option ⬍

> Time and date received

Please explain what happened:

>

Photo Credit: *support.snapchat.com/co/harassment*

Tumblr

Tumblr's guidelines simply state that they "draw lines around a few narrowly defined but deeply important categories of content and behavior that jeopardize our users, threaten our infrastructure, and damage our community."[156]

In the event that you or someone you know is being harassed on Tumblr, you should use the email *abuse@tumblr.com* to report the situation.

Additional Tips to Keep you Safe

1. Do not post pictures wearing nametags, especially with your last name.

2. Do not post vacation departure and return dates.

3. Keep your Wi-Fi secure and password protected.

4. Do not post pictures of license plates, addresses or other personal information in the background.

5. Do not include your full name, address or birth date on your public profiles. Less is always preferable.

6. Do not post items that reveal your personal daily schedule or habits.

7. Practice safe browsing and only use secure websites. Look for "https://" when using your credit card. The "s" stands for secure.

8. Read the online privacy policies VERY carefully. Most sites describe how they use your information.

9. Select nicknames when using online interactive gaming devices including Xbox Live, Nintendo, etc.

Helpful Resources

www.helpguide.org/mental/cyber-bullying.htm

www.kidpower.org/library/article/cyber-bullying

www.cyberbullying.us/Top_Ten_Tips_Teens_Prevention.pdf

http://dailym.ai/19oa2Eg

• • • • •

*"Bullying is killing our kids.
Being different is killing our kids
and the kids who are bullying are dying
inside. We have to save our kids whether
they are bullied or they are bullying.*

They are all in pain."

CAT CORA

• • • • •

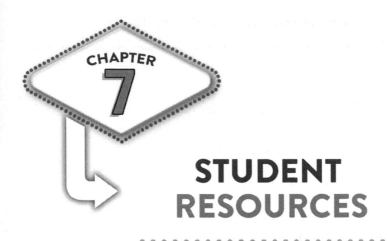

CHAPTER

7

STUDENT RESOURCES

What to Do When You Arrive on Campus

Your school is ready for you! They want to engage with you online. From the moment you apply to the time you graduate, there are great opportunities for engaging your school. Technology is also increasingly important in the classroom. Here are some tips for you to engage with your school and maximize the resources it has available to you.

1. Follow your college's main social media accounts. These will give you timely information about deadlines to look out for and major events on campus. Also, in the event of an emergency, these are often some of the channels schools use to get the word out.

2. Join your "Class of" groups and participate with your class' hashtag. Even before you get to campus, you can begin making friends and meeting people.

3. Participate in social media at new student orientation. Social media is being used more and more in orientation. Perhaps the staff is running a photo contest or a

scavenger hunt. These are great ways to get to know the campus and your fellow students.

(4) Find out what hashtags are used on campus. Pay attention to the hashtags that students use. You're entering into a new culture and you can find out a lot by just "listening" online.

(5) Figure out what questions are best asked in person versus online. Because it is so easy to hop online to ask a question, many students use this method exclusively. Sometimes the answer to your question may be more complex than what can be conveyed in 140 characters or a text reply. Try to email, call or stop by the appropriate office if your question is more involved. When a staff member can engage with you and ask questions, they can sometimes surface answers and opportunities you don't even know about.

(6) Get to know the campus learning management system. Almost all campuses use some type of online software to help you access syllabi, readings and assignments. They go by many names (BlackBoard, Canvas, Moodle, etc.) but regardless of which technology your campus uses, learn the system well. Know where to find the information you need and how to use all of the features. Being a little bit proactive will help you later on in the semester.

(7) Engage with your career services office early. Much of what is discussed in this book can help you prepare for your post-college job search. Smart planning early on in your college career can help you land a job when you graduate. Going to your career services office early for help is a smart move.

Using Digital Tools to Stay In Touch With Family and Friends

It is important to explore, grow and discover new things in college, so you want to sustain relationships back home while connecting to new experiences and people. Here are a few guidelines to keep in touch with your family and/or friends back home, and how to maintain balance when you are away at school:[157]

(1) Set a few ground rules

- Identify best applications, methods and sites to stay in touch
- Think about frequency of applications e.g. Text daily, FaceTime weekly
- Establish times for quality catch ups with your parents/friends on a regular basis

(2) Categorize conversations & consider settings— although you might have family members on your social media networks, you might want to consider

- Altering the applications settings and identify content you want to be seen in your social streams
- Creating lists/groups for conversations, sharing images, or posting videos.

(3) Consider different platforms to keep in touch

- You might not be inviting your parent to Instagram or cross-posting these images to Facebook where they are—and that's ok!
- Texting applications like Group.Me allow for groups of friends to stay in touch, share photos and interact from afar

- Maybe it's time to try Skype or Google+ Hangout because you miss seeing your family dog. Identify different communication mediums to meet your needs, and branch out.

- Maybe you want share more about your college life on a blog platform like Medium. Think about ways to keep others in touch beyond a text or call.

4. Avoid over-communicating and TMI

- Just because you can text, doesn't mean you always should. Give yourself some space to grow and become independent.

- Try to avoid oversharing all that you are doing while away at school—leave some room for catching up when you are home on holiday breaks.

20 Tips to be a Video Star

It's estimated by 2017 that over 60 percent of the content we consume on our mobile devices will be video content.[158] As such, all of us will be on video, whether it is simply for a conversation with the family via video or if we are being interviewed for a job opening.

Since these videos will be archived forever, it is important for use to put our best face forward. Below are 20 tips to help you look like a professional.

Relax your face: This actually starts with the rest of your body. Make sure your hands aren't balled up and your shoulders aren't scrunched. Some people find it helpful to give a little self-massage on the temple and neck. Also, rubbing your palms together to generate warmth and placing them onto your closed eyes is another trick to help relax your face.

≡ **No. 2** ≡

Smile: specifically concentrate on raising your cheekbones. This will naturally give the illusion to the camera that your eyes are sparkling.

≡ **No. 3** ≡

Focus on yoga-esque breaths: deep and slow. This breathing technique will help relax your face and body and will also help prevent you from talking to fast.

≡ **No. 4** ≡

If being interviewed do not use normal non-verbal cues like nodding your head. This is different from a face-to-face conversion. If you nod, it appears as if you are a "know it all" and are impatient for the question. It conveys to the audience that you already know the answer. This is a difficult habit to break so you may not get it right the first few times you are on camera; but with a little practice, it will become second nature.

≡ **No. 5** ≡

When possible use a good microphone.

No. 6

Make sure the light is on your face and not behind you. Natural light is best at dawn and dusk. If you can shoot during these periods, it will make you look your best.

No. 7

Have good posture: Stand up against a wall and have your shoulders and the top of the back of your head pressed firmly against the wall and slowly walk away from the wall keeping this posture intact for the camera; feel free to go back to slouching once the lights go off!

No. 8

Overemphasize everything: your words, excitement, volume, gestures, eyes, etc. Do not shout as if you are scolding a misbehaving dog (see #2 about being relaxed), but you need to project as if you are on stage performing a play. The first time I saw Magic Johnson being interviewed, I thought why is he shouting instead of talking in his normal voice? Then I found out the first few times I saw myself interviewed—if you are talking in your normal tone, you come across as drab and unexcited. If the bubbly Magic Johnson has to take it up a notch to look excited on film, then we all need to!

Be concise: If you are filming your own video, make it less than two minutes. If you are being interviewed, answer the question with your most powerful statement first. If it appears the interviewer wants more than you can go to the second and third most powerful points.

Sit on your tails: If you are wearing a suit jacket, tuck the tails of your coat under your behind and place your sitting bones firmly on them. This will give a nice line on your shoulders.

Make-up: If offered HD make-up, accept it. I know this will be tough for guys at first; but if you do not have it, you can look tired, shiny and old on HD. If you are at home, apply base make-up with a brush—this will dramatically reduce shine and lines. If you are like me and do not have base make-up lying around, use a cotton swap to go over your face quickly to at least remove the oil and dirt.

Hydrate: Make sure to drink plenty of fluids beforehand. Have water nearby in case you need it. Avoid ice and sugary drinks. Sparkling water with lemon is the best.

Spend the majority of the time looking into the camera. The camera is your audience. If you are on Skype/FaceTime, do not watch your little image in the corner. Look into the camera. If you are being interviewed, ask the interviewer where you should place most of your eye contact. When you get on the television show *Ellen*, make sure you know where the various cameras are and "work" each camera. If speaking on stage and you are being recorded, ask the cinematographer where you can and can't walk to be in the light and in the frame. Make sure you play to the camera for your major points of emphasis; you can use these for your highlight reel later.

Before you begin speaking, a good trick is to hum happy birthday and then immediately say, "The rain in Spain falls mainly on the plain."

Wear clothes that you are most comfortable in—what you feel you look the best in, but do not have things that would distract [e.g. large broach, crazy tie, dress with a puffy/flowery design near the top]. If you are comfortable, then you will be confident. For David Cameron, this might be a suite with a blue tie; for Garth Brooks, it might be jeans and an open collared black shirt. Try to be consistent in what you wear on video; this makes you more memorable. Johnny Cash—the man in black, Tiger Woods—red shirt on Sundays, Gene Simmons—exercise tank top, Mark Zuckerberg—hooded sweatshirt, etc.

If you feel like you have a frog in your throat, eat some cantaloupe, as this provides soothing lubrication.

Be Yourself: The above are tips to help put your best face forward. Make sure you are yourself on camera. This can be difficult. Some speaking coaches recommend you do not use your hands, but then I paid close attention to one of the best speakers in the world, Jim Collins (Author of From Good to Great) and he definitely uses his hands. The difference was that every movement had a purpose. Hence, the use of his hands assisted his delivery rather than distract from the message. If you are going to move, move with a purpose. If you are used to speaking with your hands, then speak with your hands. If you speak with your hands, then try to make sure you raise them up so that they are in frame of the camera; the worst thing is for a finger to be occasionally flying in and out of frame. If the video is only showing your head, then try to lower your hands so they have less of a chance to fly into the frame randomly. Never have your hands block your face unless you are demonstrating being ashamed.

= *No.* **18** =

Do the courtesy of all the above when filming someone else. Make them a star and they will shine brightly on you!

= *No.* **19** =

Have Fun!

= *No.* **20** =

Do post-mortems. The beautiful thing about video is you can review. Act as if you are the head coach of the New England Patriots and review video to get an advantage. How many "um"s do you say, are you slouching, do you look better with your glasses on or off, do you say "like" or other "pet" words too often. What little quirks do you have (dropping your head, slouching your shoulders, turning your back to the audience, shifty eyes)? Review these and put them into the notes section of your phone. Review the top three quirks you have the night before giving a presentation and right before you go on stage, as this will remind you to work on them.

Some of the best you can learn from: Benjamin Zander, Dan Heath, Jim Collins, Tim Sanders, Guy Kawasaki, Andy Stanley.

Discussion Prompts for Your Organization, Class or Team

(1) Describe your digital stamp. How do you want to be remembered?

(2) Describe a time when you made an offline or online mistake. How did you correct that mistake? What did you learn from that experience?

(3) Describe a time when you made digital lemonade from digital lemons. Ownership of your mistakes is FLAWsome!

(4) Name a statistic in business, your personal life, or this book that made you say "WOW!"

(5) Assemble into teams and have each team research information on a specific sports organization, company, individual or product. Each team must not only present the top positive item they uncovered and the top negative item they uncovered but also develop an action plan focusing on accentuating those strengths.

(6) After completing this book, describe one thing you would change about your online presence.

(7) Break up into teams or pairs and have each team digitally research any individual or organization they hold in high regard. Sketch a digital stamp focusing on esteemed qualities and discuss possible ways to emulate those desired qualities.

Example: The American Red Cross is a non-profit organization with the following mission statement:

> "The American Red Cross prevents and alleviates human suffering in the face of emergencies by mobilizing the power of volunteers and the generosity of donors."[159]

Ways to emulate: The American Red Cross uses Twitter to promote individual success stories of people doing good. I too can do good and will take five minutes per day to pay it forward and post positive words about people who have nurtured and supported me.

· · · · ·

"Individual commitment to a group effort—that is what makes a team work, a company work, a society work, a civilization work."

VINCE LOMBARDI

· · · · ·

GENERAL QUIZ

1. When you make a mistake online or offline, the best course of action is:

   a. Delete any mention of the mistake and maintain a low profile.

   b. Attempt to hide the mistake and refute all accusations.

   c. "Spin" the story or shift blame.

   d. Immediately and publicly accept responsibility for the mistake and describe the steps you are taking to rectify the mistake.

2. True or False: To encourage online simplicity, all users of social media sites must have multiple accounts for each site.

   ❏ True
   ❏ False

3. What rule should you follow when posting around sensitive topics including religion and politics?

   a. Keep your argument strictly emotional. Strong emotion demonstrates your passion.

   b. Present factual information and avoid combative dialogue.

   c. Vent your strong disapproval of someone's posting around these topics.

   d. Always write the post in order to convert someone to your way of thinking.

4. **When emotionally upset it is best to:**

   a. Post everything you are thinking as quickly as possible before you lose your strong emotion.

   b. Breathe deeply, count to 10, and then post.

   c. Call a friend and shriek your anger.

   d. Cancel your service provider.

5. **When you see a negative post about yourself or your organization's service, the best approach is:**

   a. Acknowledge the correct statements and apologize for any errors.

   b. Ignore the post.

   c. State that the negative post is incorrect but do not provide details.

   d. Post negative comments about the person who posted the remarks.

6. **When an online series of comments becomes emotionally heated, it is best to:**

   a. Win the argument with sarcastic comments.

   b. Breathe deeply and wait for your emotions to calm down before responding in a professional manner.

   c. Ignore the comments and stop posting any replies.

   d. Post a nasty comment on Twitter.

7. **The art of being "FLAWsome" involves:**

   a. Acknowledging your mistake or flaw while identifying steps to correct that error.

   b. Purchasing expensive dental equipment.

   c. Pointing out your competitors' flaws.

   d. Assuming an arrogant manner especially when you know you made a mistake.

8. **Topics that become heated quickly include:**

   a. Politics

   b. Religion

   c. Sexual Orientation

   d. All of the above

9. **The new rules of reputation are important for:**

   a. Executives

   b. Teenagers

   c. Employees

   d. Politicians

   e. All of the Above

10. **Often what gets people into trouble isn't the actual crime committed, but the:**

    a. Cover-up

    b. Technology

    c. Smoking gun

    d. Money involved

Answers to Quiz:
1. d 2. b 3. b 4. b 5. a 6. b 7. a 8. d 9. e/f 10. b

QUIZ FOR ATHLETIC TEAMS

1. **If you have a problem with your coach, the best step is:**

    a. Post the issue on Twitter before speaking with your coach.

    b. Talk privately with your coach about the issue.

    c. Tell everyone you know to get his or her advice.

    d. Talk to the press.

2. **True or False: You should constantly update the status of an injury or personal issue on social media.**

    ❑ True
    ❑ False

3. **To help motivate your team and "psych-out" an upcoming opponent you should:**

    a. Post inflammatory comments on social media sites.

    b. Post the wide point spread in favor of your team on Twitter.

    c. Motivate your teammates inside the locker room or during practice.

    d. Post unflattering remarks about specific players on the opposing team.

4. **If you are being hazed or bullied by a teammate, you should:**

   a. Ask that teammate(s) to stop.

   b. Approach the captain of the team and ask for assistance.

   c. Approach and discuss the issue with the coach.

   d. All of the above in this order.

   e. None of the above.

5. **When someone posts negative comments about you personally, it is best to:**

   a. Ignore the post or respond in a calm, focused manner.

   b. Blame others and minimize your involvement.

   c. Find something negative to say about that person.

   d. Post the scenario on Facebook.

6. **When an online series of comments becomes emotionally heated, it is best to:**

   a. Win the argument with unkind or sarcastic remarks.

   b. Breathe deeply, count to 10, and then post responsibly.

   c. Have your boyfriend or girlfriend posting from his or her own account in your defense.

   d. Unfriend that person.

7. Family, friends, boyfriends or girlfriends must understand:

    a. Negative posts or comments about the team or an opponent are a direct reflection on you and your team.

    b. Negative posts or comments can result in strained relationships with the press and the coach.

    c. Pointing out the flaws of your competitors is completely unacceptable.

    d. All of the above.

8. Game plans should be:

    a. Kept to yourself.

    b. Shared with friends and family.

    c. Posted to social media so you can attract more followers.

    d. Disclosed to friendly press member who travel with the team.

9. Participation on social media during the season is:

    a. A necessity

    b. A privilege

    c. Best used during the game

10. **Often what gets people into trouble isn't actually the crime committed, but the:**

    a. Money involved

    b. Cover-up

    c. Technology

    d. Smoking gun

11. **The best way to increase my value with pro scouts via social media is:**

    a. Post three to five times per day.

    b. Post the reasons you would make a great pro.

    c. Use social media to compare and contrast your athletic abilities with current professional athletes.

    d. Be genuine, interact with fans in a professional manner and work hard.

    e. Interact and "friend" professional agents via social media.

12. **When is it appropriate to use profane language or racial slurs in a joking manner?**

    a. With teammates because this type of banter bonds the team.

    b. With select friends who understand the context and your sense of humor.

    c. With the opposite sex.

    d. Never.

13. **The best way to increase popularity and gain followers on Twitter is:**

    a. Show a genuine interest in others and try to provide them value.

    b. Do something controversial.

    c. Post frequently about anything that crosses your mind.

    d. Tweet comments about your teammates or coaches.

14. **If you are not getting sufficient playing time, you should:**

    a. Lobby for more playing time via social media.

    b. Convince several close friends to post your displeasure on social media.

    c. Discuss your concerns with the coaches in a private conversation.

    d. Become friends with the press and describe your displeasure in great detail so they can write an article.

15. **If an attractive person flirts with you online, you should:**

    a. Use social media to develop the relationship before meeting in person.

    b. Send impressive information about yourself.

    c. Meet in person after you check their digital profile.

    d. Take a snapshot and forward to your best friend.

16. **If you find reading comments about yourself on social media is negatively affecting your athletic performance or hurting your class work, you should:**

    a. Take a break from social media until the season or semester is over.

    b. Pay external social media agencies or consultants to manage your accounts.

    c. Hire a sports agent to help you manage your life.

    d. Watch videos on TMZ.

Answers to Quiz:

1. b 2. b (false) 3. c 4. d 5. a 6. b 7. d 8. a
9. b 10. b 11. d 12. d 13. a 14. c 15. c 16. a

DIGITAL STAMPS

A Digital Stamp is a permanent collection and culmination of your digital footprints and digital shadows. Your digital stamp matters 5 seconds from now, 5 years from now, 50 years from now, and 500 years from now.

I asked individuals and companies to submit the digital STAMP they want to leave on this world. Here are some responses. You submit your own at equalman@equalman.com. We will absolutely add more to the next edition. If your stamp didn't make this edition, it can certainly be in the next edition. Heartfelt thanks to my loyal supporters; this book would not exist without you! As for me, my desired STAMP is:

"Be a Digital Dale Carnegie by motivating others to their best life, leadership & legacy. Honor my family & God."

@equalman

"She inspired people to dream big. She empowered educators to disrupt the status quo & create an experience where all students can thrive."

Courtney O'Connell (@CourtOconnell)

"Inspiring others to be digital adventurers, vanguards, and change agents."

Paul Gordon Brown (@paulgordonbrown)

"Provide a digital remix to empower the leaders of the 21st century."

Josie Ahlquist (@JosieAhlquist)

"An early adopter, educator, & leader in digital tech in higher ed through his work at Bridgewater State, the #SAtech Unconference, & ACPA."

Ed Cabellon (@EdCabellon)

"She considered transformational experiences, feminism, and vulnerability central to her work in higher education and student affairs."

Heather Shea Gasser (@heathergasser)

"Digital immortality? Am ambivalent. Today."

Ana M. Martinez-Aleman (@AnaMMartinez1)

"Positive disruptor, leading and advocating for social and digital change. Bring it on!"

Julie Payne-Kirchmeier (@jpkirchmeier)

"Challenge others to realize their self-determined greatness. Progressive leader, educator, role model. Interesting, interested and proud dad."

Tony Doody (@TonyDoody)

"Her grandmother often told her 'You've got to care!' And boy, does she ever. She is funny, candid, bright. But most of all, she cares."

Carey Loch (@CareyLoch)

"Expand what we know to change how we live. Make today better than yesterday by embracing the questions and learning with each other."

Rachel Luna (@RachelHLuna)

"Do what you love. ALWAYS. Talk about it. Share your passion. Find your online community. Eventually the rest of the world will come around."

Laura Pasquini (@LauraPasquini)

"Living her life truly and deeply and empowering others to do the same."

Kristen Abell (@Kristen_Abell)

"A digital resister of ideologies that divide us. Her "we" is big."

Cindi Love (@drcindilove)

"Exploring possibilities, putting useful apps to work every day, and contributing to the body of digital knowledge."

Margie Putnam

"My legacy, he loved Jesus, loved his family, great family man & wonderful businessman. In that order."

Greg Baily @bigtimemarketer

"The web is my playground."

@kwerner

"That I made life fun."

@phylliskhare

"To have made a difference to people I touch."

@thelinkedinman

"Help Higher Education Sector understand how social media can improve customer service/relationship management."

@davidgirlinguk

"I want every one of my academic papers and studies and lectures to be accessible and available to all (+free)"

@JohnGirdwood

"She was real. She cared. She connected!"

@SCMSJanine

"I want my legacy to be a rich narrative of connections, experience and expertise."

@TSCollier217

"Compassionate connector, insatiably curious, convinced sleep is overrated."

@ScratchMM

"10 years from now I would like people to see how geeky I was in 2013."

@JeanRicher

"I would like my digital legacy to be an understanding of how digital is part of everything but is nothing on its own"

@SimonSalento

"Always cared about others well being and made it a point to put others in front of himself"

@joshharcus

"Impacted how teachers & parents embrace educating children on building relationships & protecting their personal brands using social media"

Scott Wild

"We listened because he did."

@arnoldtijerina7

"She didn't "talk at," she "listened to" and engaged with her audience on a more personable level."

@PamSahota

"Life is full of seasons, but at the end of mine, I want others to find that I spoke for those who couldn't speak for themselves."

@JanieSikes

"Be Real. Live your passion. Stay present. Never let your mind second guess your heart."

@springboardw

"I impacted other lives in a positive way. I was passionate about life and lived with a true sense of gratitude. I created my own path."

Jason DeAmato

"Andrew was a great father and manager. His specialty was growing online businesses in good and bad economic times. He made everyone laugh."

Andrew Artemenko

"Develop my business and career. It's my digital CV…"

@paulpingles

"Create awareness for, visibility of & support to people in need who are less fortunate than us!"

@jonrpeters

"He challenged the established norms in the realm of digital marketing to facilitate growth of companies he is associated with."

Arun Varma

"Helping broaden narrow minds."

@earthianne

"He believed in the ability of mankind to change the World."
Jean Baptiste

"He loved and invested in a younger generation, encouraging them to be remarkable for the glory of God."
@alvinreid

"I'm the tweep behind 'The Greatest Customer Service Story Ever Told'."
@JillianMktng

"He was a relational architect who helped Higher Education embrace social media as a new "normal" while wearing sweatervests."
John Hill

"He invested his life into mine, taught me to live wide awake and step into the fullest and best version of myself."
Scott Schimmel

"He inspired and entertained, he blessed many, he was a success as a man."
Ryan Bethea

"Strived to promote genuine values in work, family, friendship, love and everyday life."
Jason Rubley "Rubes"

"I follow the creator, servant, CrossFiter, firefighter, helper, Student, Tennessean, technology enthusiasts, leader."
@C_RSmith

"Inspired others to live a great story through healthy living, love of family, community service and a sense of adventure."
Shanna Kurpe

"He was great in virtue."
Maciej Łobza

"I hope to they see how to alter their children's legacy by learning how to leave the planet better than they found it."
Kristina Summers

"Like Kipling, I know something of the things which are underneath, and of the things which are beyond the frontier."
Jim Nico

"Layne continues to spread her love of humanity through her works and writings. She lives happily with her wife of 110 years and their dog."
Layne Holley

"I overcame the pain of losing an infant and was a loved and loving father and husband. And, I gave my boys the gift of writing. Beautifully."
Mark Irvine

"Known for artistic expression, Laurie developed & nurtured relationships & influenced action & change by listening & sharing relevant & compelling information."
Laurie Wakefield

"We will transform collaboration in Brazil through the power of education, technology and fun!"
Luiz Irumé & Sâmara Irumé, E-continuus Inc.

"Christoph showed that communication is happiness and the essential thing in life."
Christoph Jeschke

"A freedom fighter who believed everyone is a leader. She encouraged others to stand up, do something, be meaningful."
Nancy Beth Guptill

"She proved that kindness and caring is the true key to success."
Katelyn Auclair

"She brought genetic carrier status out of the closet."
Jane Belland Karwoski – MyBlueGenome

"A freedom fighter who believed everyone is a leader. She encouraged others to stand up, do something, be meaningful."
@SweetMarketing

"She made all the little things count, no matter how small, happy is happy."
@sarahJAYYallday

"Enabling footprints to broaden the reach & access in closing the digital & social divide."
@mwthomasSCRM

"She inspired and empowered generations of authors."
@LisaTener

"He turned an obsession with Social Media into a series of successful businesses, and he had a BLAST every step of the way."
Michael McClure

"A leader who inspired others to create opportunities and act based on their passion in life."
@akassab

"That I helped out people who were in need and all the different organizations I was involved in and all the good I had done around the world."
Cole Menzel

"That I became a successful Music Supervisor, I'd want my life to be reflected as a good one. Someone who achieved what they wanted."

Erin Zins @erinzins

"I'd want my digital legacy to sum up my life. It would be really interesting to just look back at anyone, and see what their lives like."

Brandon Wilton

"A really good teacher."

Megan Peters

"For helping people in some way, like giving up something important to me or giving my life for someone to live or prosper better."

Jason Ratcliff

"I would want it to talk about the things that I accomplished, my family, the people who were close to me."

Boochi Kashinkunti

"That I loved my family more than they will ever know and I was pretty good at writing IEP's."

Vicki Peterman

"1. I did not do something just because everyone else did. 2. When I am tagged in photos, I look like a swamp monster. 3. I dressed FABULOUSLY."

Abby Lawley

"The hard work I put into becoming the person I am today and that it allows me and my friends to look back and be proud of who we were."

Brock Kamrath

"An article about me graduating from Mizzou, my work in the field of nuclear power, and solve the energy crisis that we will continue to face."

Jessie Jennings

"To show that I am a kind and selfless person, that I rather think of others than myself. All in all for have a big heart."

Meghan McMurray

"That I made a difference in peoples' lives. That I did all I could to help others who couldn't help themselves and I succeeded."

Tricia Morgan

"My digital legacy stamp would simply be "Grace Gollon is awesome.""

Grace Gollon

"A website with a short bio about me, and how I started a nationally-known organization."

Leah Mergen (@missLMergen)

"A woman who loved God, her family, was blessed beyond her wildest dreams and was a blessing to others."

Julie Zara

"Tyler was loyal to his friends and family. He loved where he came from (Riverton IL). He was patriotic, happy and thankful for living in the USA!"

Tyler Curry (@Tyler_Curry89)

"She's a leader that's purposeful, positive and present and because of that she was able to empower thousands of women to live their dream."

Julie Timm

"A strong woman who survived many tests in her lifetime. She beat breast cancer and selflessly participated in research for The Cure. She gave all that she had to her family & friends. She loved unconditionally and was loved endlessly."
Mary Tolley

"As a microlending nonprofit, PeopleFund would like to be remembered as being a 'hand up, not hand out.'"
Miku Sakamoto

"She was a caring individual who used her creative gifts and talents to help others!"
Jennifer Frey

"She inspired people to think big and achieve things they never thought possible. She revolutionized education."
Courtney O'Connell (@CourtOconnell)

"Glass half-full kind of girl. I want her on my team. Always growing and learning. She helped me (fill in the blank). Let's shake it up."
Katie Beals (@katiebeals)

"Absolutely nothing. The world is the playground of the living. I hope they enjoy it as much as I did."
John Cimmino

"Passionate, Nerdy, Student Affairs Professional, Loves public speaking and helping students at every turn. D&D, MMOs, books, Whedonite."
Michael Ambyth

"Cynthia engages people in social justice through media, technology and artistic expression in Higher Ed & Student Affairs communities."
Cynthia Kaselis (@CynthiaKaselis)

"My ABCs: Always be part of something greater than yourself. Bring out the best in others. Create & conquer. #Rutgers #JerseyStrong #highered"

Sandra Golis (@SandraG1117)

"I am a Student Affairs professional, world traveler and avid knitter. I want to make the world a better place one stitch at a time."

Kolrick Greathouse (@KolGreat)

"Hard work pays off and a little faith goes a long way. I've loved,lost, and made mistakes but I LIVED! I love people. Jersey Strong-Go RU!"

Amber McNeil (@LeonaSp10)

"That I've made the world a little bit happier through my efforts. Happiness through fulfillment, laughter and connections."

Dustin Ramsdell (@highered_geek)

"Dedicated father and college professional that solved the problems of the world through authentic helpfulness, one college student at a time."

Bobby Bullard (@BBullard7)

"I want individuals to change the way they think about finance and economics and apply practical finance tips to their lives."

Sagar Lakhani (@sman9000)

"Someone who harnessed the power of online professionally and personally, embraced the digital evolution and rolled with its daily changes."

Peter Hughes (@hughespjh)

"I'd like to be remembered as a true professional, objective, dedicated to my craft, who treated people well and added value to their lives."

Steve Amoia (@worldfootballcm)

"God, country & family. Happy 2 know @equalman—a great thought leader & person. Love to Mary-Beth, Lucia, Eva & Mica, & my brother Glenn!"

Stephen Selby (@StephenFSelby)

"Tim helps churches grow through communicating better."

Tim Peters (@timrpeters)

"Number crunching photographer who loves riding my bicycle really, really fast. I live with MS and write about it on The Lesion Journals."

Christie Germans (@lesionjournals)

"I hope people find a legacy. Family members can look back and know exactly who I was. That the internet showcases a snapshot of life today."

Lisa Simonson (@PRladyLisa)

"I don't define myself solely by what I do or what I have achieved. I love my life and I love what I do. Each day more of what I do reflects what I love to do."

Melissa Silva (@ChiaMelly)

"Follower of Jesus. Love of my wife, kids, family & friends. Big time business leader, marketer & innovator. Global education philanthropist."

Greg Bailey (@bigtimemarketer)

"A digital native who loves connecting with people. Always learning new stuff and likes helping internet startups & businesses."

Neeraj Thakur (@NeerajT4)

"As a Nara-born editor who created useful English learning materials for Japanese and also as a tour guide for foreigners coming to Japan."

Yusuke Takeuchi (@sosorasora)

"Evidence of his work expanding the understanding between technology and education all while making sure students were achieving their goals."

Josh Kohnert (@JoshKohnert)

"Next generation leader that equips & empowers leaders to leverage today's tools, trends & talent to thrive tomorrow."

Ryan Jenkins (@theRyanJenks)

"True nobility is not about being better than anyone else; it's about being better than you used to be."

Rod Ponce (@rodponce)

"Connector, Empathy driven, Humane."

Vikram Mekala (@mekalav)

"Rolled with the #Apple Crew while still being able to hang with the #Google Gang, Digital Ninja, Author of @ichurch-method"

Jason Caston (@jasoncaston)

"I'd like people (or robots) in 2113 to find a connected, curious, compassionate Molly who eventually learned to express herself in 140 chara (intentionally cut off)"

Molly Rucki (@mollyrucki)

"Social & Digital Marketing Strategist, Marketing Data Scientist, Competitive Runner, Assistant Professor, University of Missouri—St. Louis"

Perry D. Drake (@pddrake)

"I tried to help people in every way I could. I spread the truth and loved my family."
Jason Bhatti (@bhattibytes)

"To be a motivator and connector of small business owners increasing their revenues while supporting God's work."
Mike Saunders (@marketinghuddle)

"A true community developer—at home, in my neighbourhood, at work, online. One coffee mug at a time."
Lindsey Fair (@lindseyfair)

"@tamcdonald, aka Tim McDonald: Builder of communities, not networks. Teacher via being a perpetual student. Be happy. Do good. #ArtOfWork"
Tim McDonald (@tamcdonald)

"Won't be satisfied until we actually change something about the world, make it better."
Brian Reich (@brianreich)

"Jordan loved life, and cared passionately about humanity. He was loved by many for enabling them to follow their dreams."
Jordan Skoe (@JordanSkole)

"Dr. Syb truly lived, loved & learned. Her legacy of passion, engagement & wisdom remains contagious. Catch & share it."
Sybril Bennett (@drsyb)

"Family matters most. Lots of love to our family Helga, Karl, Óli, Sibbi, Grímur, Kalli and their families. Gummi and family."
Gudmundur Karl Karlsson (@gummikalli)

"Author of the #1 selling LinkedIn book The Power Formula for LinkedIn Success, LinkedIn Trainer, Speaker, Consultant, CPA...love cat."
Wayne Breitbarth (@waynebreitbarth)

"I hope folks would discover I'm a teacher, philanthropist, recognized speaker, business builder and great dad and husband."
MIke Merrill (@MikeDMerrill)

"Business thinker who tries to democratize access to opportunity."
Dorie Clark (@dorieclark)

"Dependable, Honest, Respectful, Trustworthy, Kind, Generous, Intelligent. Mother, Wife, Sister, Daughter. Passion for life, music, art, peace."
April McCormack (@ivycoils)

"Paul was a really nice guy who made a difference in the lives of the individuals that he met."
Paul Goldenberg (@bluefrogpaul)

"Always present, prepared and passionate about work, friends and family."
Nancy Kohutek

"President and Co-Founder of pidalia & racut — Mad Man, Speaker, Technologist, and Sushi Connoisseur."
Scott Dubois (@ScottDubois)

"Builder of marketing ideas that irrevocably connect people and brands."
Chris Perkins (@TopherPerkins)

"I hope that I've made a positive impact on people helping find their passions in life, and had some fun along the way."
Dustin Ramsdell (@highered_geek)

"I hope that, 100 years from now, my online legacy will provide an accurate and consistent picture of who I was - both online and IRL."
Tyrone Hooge (@tyronehooge)

"Proud father of Sara, Sindri and Sunna. Solution designer focused on optimizing businesses with innovative technology. Loves a challenge."
Ingólfur Þorsteinsson (@IngolfurTh)

"They were honest and fair and raised a good family."
Philip Kiger

"Chandler Vreeland"
Chandler Vreeland

"Aproveite a vida! =)"
Leonardo Magalhaes

"Christie is a number crunching photographer who loves riding her bicycle really, really fast and lives with Multiple Sclerosis (MS)."
Christie Germans (@lesionjournals)

"I found my passion late in life—teaching. So I hope my digital stamp will show that I helped my students find their passion and encouraged them to reach their full potential."
Dale Blasingame (@daleblasingame)

"A leader who inspired others to create opportunities and act based on their passion in life."
Alex Kassab (@akassab)

"Hopefully not too much cat content I posted ;)"
David Redelberger (@davidfromkassel)

"Proud Mother of Darcy and Shea who made the world a better place by just being themselves."
Nikki Moran

"Someone who started 3D character animation in Mauritius; someone who started the first 3D Animation Training in Mauritius; an entrepreneur who always tried new things, and was never scared of the uncertainties of life."
Satyen Bhujun

"Create a better world by working quietly behind the scenes to connect people, spark ideas & catalyze change under the guise of serendipity."
Jennifer Barrett (@jenbarrett)

"IF OPPORTUNITY DOESN'T KNOCK, BUILD A DOOR."
Piers Brown (@bohonews)

"I love web development, social media, cats and music. I like my online world to cover all of those things."
Jess Wearn (@helloitsjess)

"Many moments of laughter, leadership and love."
Lizzie Williams (@LLLizzie)

"I would hope that people find that I created more than consumed, helped more than hindered, loved, took risks, made mistakes and learned."
Dave Banas (@davebanas)

"Happy 2 know @equalman—a true thought leader—and to help kickstart this book! Love to MB, Lucia, Eva, Mica & my brother Glenn!"
Stephen Selby (@stephenfselby)

"@arnobiomorelix, social entrepreneur from PESSOA Institute, an organization teaching entrepreneurship to remote communities in South America"
Arnobio Morelix (@arnobiomorelix)

"I hope people will find that I found my passion, loved my job, worked hard & made a difference in higher education & a student's experience."

Cortney Brewer (@Cortbrew)

"A great husband, dad and leader who loves family, the auto industry and science, technology, engineering & math education."

Mark Johnson

"Connector of remarkable strategies, ideas, business and people...Passionate about family, an active lifestyle and giving back."

Patrick Sitkins (@patricksitkins)

"I would like people to find photos of my family, friends and beloved dog Bentley. I believe pictures and videos speak louder than words."

Stephanie Corritori (@scorritoricbsi)

• • • • •

"The supreme quality for leadership is unquestionably integrity. Without it, no real success is possible, no matter whether it is on a section gang, a football field, in an army, or in an office."

DWIGHT D. EISENHOWER

• • • • •

STUDENT SUCCESS STORIES

The following are stories about inspiring students who are thriving in the digital age. These are personal insights from individuals who have achieved success in the digital age as college students. Their personal stories will inspire you to achieve your best in whatever it is you choose to pursue. Each of them included their Twitter handle so that our readers can reach out to them with questions or just to connect.

Megan Gebhart
When you get lots of clicks, you're doing something right

Writing and social media came easy to Michigan State Alum, Megan Gebhart. During her senior year at MSU, she challenged herself to have one cup of coffee with one thought leader once a week for an entire year and write about it. She named her project, *52 Cups of Coffee: a yearlong experiment in caffeine and conversation.*

As a marketing student, she gained 500-600 Twitter followers when she worked for the Michigan State Alumni Association. This is what inevitably catapulted her idea into reality. Megan said, "Somewhere, someone posted my link on *metafilter.com* which was this big online community & one day I was looking through my analytics traffic and it was through the roof with clicks." It was from here that Megan's journey began and took her to 29 cities across 7 countries.

She set her sights high for her conversations. Through the use of social media and by asking thought leaders if they could help a college student by way of a few minutes over coffee, she found success. She was able to chat with the founder of Apple (Steve Wozniak), the top marketing guru in the world (Seth Godin), Michigan State basketball coach Tom Izzo, innovators at Nike, the creator of *Shark Week*, a WWII veteran, college presidents and beyond.

By constructing a strong online identity with *52 Cups*, Megan's digital footprint has carried her through a tremendous amount of opportunity to meet new people and form new friendships. Both online and offline, Megan's journey led to her first job out of school at a well-known Silicon Valley tech company. It also accelerated her personal development. Reflecting back on her experience as a college student, Megan realizes that her plans had changed, albeit in a positive way. She said, "My original plan was to get a job... because of 52 Cups and my online following it totally changed the trajectory ... the first year and half caught me off guard in a good way."

Gebhart indicates the best way she has built a strong digital reputation has been to always be aware of her audience and connect with them whenever possible. Because Megan has "... a bigger audience and people might misconstrue things" she really focuses on writing quality content so that, "other things I post are always in alignment." Gebhart's blog was so successful that it was picked up by a publisher and turned into a book titled: *52 Cups of Coffee: Inspiring and insightful stories for navigating life's uncertainties.*

@megangebhart

Channing Moreland & Makenzie Stokel
Getting support validates your passion

Roommates Channing Moreland and Makenzie Stokel's passion is music. Together, they infused their passions and lessons learned from their studies in Entrepreneurship and Music Business and set sail to make an impact in the music community of Nashville. It started with an idea. Channing said, "... we went for it ... we put on our own music festival for college students called "Porchfest" and... we brought about 500 people to it."

The success of Porchfest is what inspired their current business endeavor called What's Hubbin'—an online platform that posts information for music lovers to stay up to date with live music performances in Nashville. Makenzie believes that posts should be, "good quality. [We] never want to have anyone doubt our information. It takes one time for someone to doubt our info and never return to our site." When it comes to digital reputation both women agree—it's important to be professional in order to move forward. Regarding the success of What's Hubbin', Makenzie said, "It kind of took a while ... I sort of realized 'Wow, people are getting down with this' once we started getting a lot of great feedback. It's a dream come true."

It has taken more than a dream for the What's Hubbin' co-founders to turn their idea into a successful reality. To balance time between studies and business management, the women use a lot of their weekend time to put into their music tech company. Due to lots of hard work with marketing and the planning of music events, What's Hubbin has generated up to 3,000 active members

@WhatsHubbin

Tim Downey
Learning from mistakes and benefiting from mentors

As a serial entrepreneur, Belmont University student Tim Downey has learned many lessons. During his first major business of an outdoor clothing company, Tim said, "It failed miserably and it was because I didn't do my homework. I messed up on my inventory." Now, as a business entrepreneurship major, Tim is doing homework while going confidently in the direction of his new digital marketing business with the help of relevant courses and meaningful mentorships.

Tim's company Picd.us, a social media marketing site, was largely influenced by his experience as an intern with technology company, BKON. As a Director of Entrepreneurial Initiatives, he learned about "blue tooth technology that tracks usage of mobile devices. All of the workers have at one point owned a business ... it's helped out tremendously with my business." With the help of mentors and advisory board members who are invaluable to Tim's growth, he has been able to create a site that aligns itself with product placement via social media

The success of Picd.us can be credited to the digital reputation Tim has built for himself and Picd.us. The company's twitter account and his blog, *Lessons from a First Time CEO*, has helped to gather the attention of many potential clients. To date, Tim has been able to score partnerships with small businesses, four U.S company partnerships, and one international partnership.

@TimPDowney

Kaitlyn Rajner

Students really care about branding themselves

As a student leader at the State University of New York, Oswego, Kaitlyn has leveraged her experience in public relations to its full potential. She has held multiple internships relating to her studies and constantly keeps her social media presence relevant and professional. She is the student project lead for the *Digital Dirt Squad*—a peer education group that teaches students about social media, digital reputation, and the importance of managing one's own digital footprint.

Kaitlyn's responsibilities revolve around helping her peers create a positive digital footprint. This includes having one-on-one lessons with students about self-assessing their online identity, visiting classrooms to help peers build LinkedIn profiles, and teaching others how to create websites.

She realized how important the *Digital Dirt Squad* was when, "I presented to a COM 490 class (seniors only) and the students asked so many important questions...the students asked about how to brand themselves and create professional platforms, so I realized that what I was saying was really registering with them." Kaitlyn even utilizes her social media lessons for herself. When it comes to digital reputation, she said, "...[it] has helped me make connections with a few people that I would like to work for. My bosses at my internship follow me on Twitter, so maintaining a positive presence is necessary."

@kaitlyn_rajner

#CarryThatWeight:
One voice can spark a nationwide conversation

A Columbia University student turned her sexual assault on campus into her senior thesis project entitled *Mattress Performance: Carry That Weight.* By pledging to carry a dormitory mattress throughout campus until her rapist is either expelled or leaves the University, the student gained nationwide attention. Various media outlets, universities, political parties, and nonprofit organizations quickly became involved in the conversation surrounding sexual assault and domestic violence.

In response, student activists created a #carrythatweight online campaign that called for a day of action on October 29, 2014. With the help of partnerships from nonprofit organizations Hollaback! and Rhize, and student organizations *Carrying The Weight Together* and *No Red Tape,* up to 130 campuses were inspired to participate in the day of action and nearly 10,000 people attended the Facebook event. Students from all over the globe were carrying dormitory mattresses on campus in solidarity with the Columbia University student and the countless other victims of sexual assault around the world.

The power of online advocacy has a global reach and massive potential to enact change. When the student activists put a spotlight on campus sexual assault, pressure was put on decision makers to act. As of January 2015, the Department of Education's Office for Civil Rights is investigating Columbia University and 94 other Universities for violations of Title IX —a federal law that prohibits discrimination of sex in education institutions.

@CarryTogether

GLOSSARY

CATFISH: Someone who uses social media and other digital tools to create a false persona. Typically used to attract online romances. For example, the user posts a beautiful picture and an impressive biography under a false name.

Former Notre Dame Linebacker and NFL player Manti Te'o indicated he was a victim of catfishing. [155]

"Catfish" is a 2010 movie that tells the story of a young man who develops an online relationship with a woman who is vastly different from her Facebook profile.[156]

The origin of the term could stem from the movie or the restaurant practice of substituting a cheaper fish in place of customer's more expensive selection.

CYBERBULLY: To tease, insult or make fun of another person online. The intent is to destroy the target's reputation. Cyberbullying is often considered a criminal offense. Offline bullying laws apply to online behavior.

DIGTIAL FOOTPRINT: Everything you post about yourself online. Examples include status update, blog post, photo/video upload, text, tweet, etc.

DIGITAL LEGACY: (See Digital Stamp)

DIGITAL SHADOWS: The items other people post about you. This includes your online and offline actions. Almost every person and organization has a digital shadow, even if he or she does not use online tools.

DIGITAL STAMP: A permanent collection and culmination of your digital footprints and digital shadows. Your digital stamp matters 5 seconds from now, 5 years from now, 50 years from now and 500 years from now.

FLAWsome: Something or someone who is fantastic yet flawed. This can be a person, company, product, organization or object. FLAWsome combines the words Flaws and Awesome. As a company or individual, you can prove how awesome you are when you make a mistake and take actions to correct that mistake.

Non-business example: Chicago's Wrigley Field is old with small uncomfortable seats, insufficient parking and overly expensive drinks, yet it is a totally FLAWsome ballpark.

POST-IT FORWARD: Similar to the offline act of paying it forward in which an individual performs an act of kindness without expecting something in return such as paying for a stranger's expired parking meter. Online examples include endorsing someone on LinkedIn, positively posting about someone else's success on Twitter or Facebook, liking someone's post, re-tweeting, etc.

RETWEET: A retweet is a re-posting of someone else's tweet. Twitter's retweet feature helps you and others quickly share that tweet with all your followers. Sometimes people type RT at the beginning of a tweet to indicate they are re-posting someone else's content. This is not an official Twitter command or feature but signifies the person is quoting another user's Tweet. It is analogous to forwarding an email.

TROLL: Online user who posts inflammatory posts on message boards, blogs, comment section or product reviews in order to incite controversy and argument. Their arguments and comments are often off-topic.

Wikipedia definition: In Internet slang, a troll (/ tro l/, / tr l/) is a person who sows discord on the Internet by starting arguments or upsetting people, by posting inflammatory, extraneous or off-topic messages in an online community (such as a forum, chat room or blog), either accidentally or with the deliberate intent of provoking readers into an emotional response or of otherwise disrupting normal on-topic discussion.

TWEETING: The act of posting digital messages in a 140 character or less format on the popular micro-blogging platform Twitter.

• • • • •

"Integrity does not come in degrees— low, medium or high. You either have integrity or you do not."

TONY DUNGY

• • • • •

NOTES

[1] Leslie Meredith, "Internet Safety for Kids: Almost All Children Under 2 Have A Digital Footprint," *Huffington Post via AVG Study,* January 10, 2013, http://www.huffingtonpost.com/2013/01/10/children-internet-safety_n_2449721.html

[2] "Tweeter's Remorse? Some Users Regret What They've Shared on Social Media," *CBSNewYork,* July 29, 2013, http://newyork.cbslocal.com/2013/07/29/tweeters-remorse-some-users-regret-what-theyve-shared-on-social-media/

[3] http://www.careerbuilder.com/share/aboutus/pressreleasesdetail.aspx?sd=6%2F26%2F2014&id=pr829&ed=12%2F31%2F2014

[4] Albright-Hanna, Adam. "Some Teens Kept Sexually Harassing This Young Journalist. So She Humiliated the Hell Out of Them." GOOD Magazine. N.p., 01 Dec. 2014. http://magazine.good.is/articles/fighting-back-the-trolls

[5] John Greathouse, "Eight Startup Tips From Mark Zuckerberg," *INFOCHACHKIE,* January 23, 2012, http://infochachkie.com/8-startup-tips-mark-zuckerberg/

[6] http://www.forbes.com/sites/travisbradberry/2014/10/08/multitasking-damages-your-brain-and-career-new-studies-suggest/

[7] Jobvite. "Jobvite Social Recruiting Survey." Jobvite 2014 Job Seeker Nation: Mobility In The Workforce Study (n.d.): n. pag. Aug. 2014. Jobvite Survey 2014, https://www.jobvite.com/wp-content/uploads/2014/10/Jobvite_SocialRecruiting_Survey2014.pdf

[8] Ramirez, Fernando. "Social Media Screening: A Candidate's Perspective." Recruiter. N.p., 9 Oct. 2014. https://www.recruiter.com/i/social-media-screening-a-candidates-perspective/

[9] Corporation, Oracle. "Modern HR in The Cloud." Best Practices Recruiting the Right Talent (n.d.): n. pag. Oracle Human Capital Management, 2013. http://www.oracle.com/us/products/applications/human-capital-management/talent-mgmt-rec-best-practices-2157035.pdf

[10] http://www.theatlantic.com/technology/archive/2011/08/project-class-room-transforming-our-schools-for-the-future/244182/

[11] https://www.linkedin.com/static?key=pop%2Fpop_more_profile_completeness

[12] Susan Adams, "LinkedIn Got Me Two Great Jobs," *Forbes*, January 19, 2012, http://www.forbes.com/sites/susanadams/2012/01/19/true-story-linkedin-got-me-two-great-jobs/

[13] Swartz, Jonathan. "Cornell Enables Students to Apply Using LinkedIn Profiles." *USA TODAY College*. N.p., 14 July 2014. Web. 30 Jan. 2015. http://www.huffingtonpost.com/2014/11/25/yik-yak-threats-college_n_6214794.html

[14] Svokos, Alexandra. "Yik Yak Threats Lead To Charges For Students." *The Huffington Post*. TheHuffingtonPost.com, 25 Nov. 2014. Web. 30 Jan. 2015. http://www.dailytarheel.com/article/2014/11/student-arrested-after-false-bomb-threat-on-yik-yak

[15] Brown, Sarah. "Student Arrested after False Bomb Threat on Yik Yak." *The Daily Tar Heel*. N.p., 21 Nov. 2014. Web. 30 Jan. 2015. http://www.dailytarheel.com/article/2014/11/student-arrested-after-false-bomb-threat-on-yik-yak.

[16] http://www.huffingtonpost.com/2014/11/07/university-of-albany-yik-yak-threats_n_6121998.html

[17] Arnold, Van. "Arrest Made in Alleged Social Media Threat to University of Southern Mississippi." University of Southern Mississippi. N.p., 2 Oct. 2014. Web. 30 Jan. 2015. http://www.usm.edu/news/article/arrest-made-alleged-social-media-threat-university-southern-mississippi

[18] Mai Bruun Poulsen, "How a Rainbow-Oreo Sparked a Boycott and Doubled the Fan Growth," *Mndjumpers*, July 9, 2012, http://www.mind-jumpers.com/blog/2012/07/oreo-boycott/

[19] http://espn.go.com/high-school/track-and-xc/story/_/id/8010251/high-school-runner-carries-fallen-opponent-finish-line

[20] I first heard this word from Marketing Professor's Ann Handley – check out her great work!

[21] Jennifer Larsen, Maritz Research and Evolve24- Twitter Study. Rep. Maritz Research and Evolve24, September 2011, http://www.maritzresearch.com/~/media/Files/MaritzResearch/e24/ExecutiveSummaryTwitterPoll.ashx

[22] "National Stalking Awareness Month Observed in January." The Gazette-Democrat. N.p., 9 Jan. 2015. http://www.annanews.com/news/article_d33c949a-981f-11e4-8efd-73c5adfe8c95.html

[23] Kulze, Elizabeth. "Why Is Nobody Speaking Out About On-Campus Stalking?"Vocativ. N.p., 15 Jan. 2015. http://www.vocativ.com/usa/education-usa/stalking-college-campuses/

[24] Jennifer Valentino-Devries, "Hackers Leak IDs Tied to Apple Devices," *The Wall Street Journal*, September 5, 2012, http://online.wsj.com/article/SB10000872396390444301704577631721370098002.html?mod=googlenews_wsj

[25] http://www.cnn.com/2012/11/12/us/petraeus-cia-resignation/

[26] David Kirkpatrick, "The Facebook Effect," *Simon & Schuster*, February 1, 2011

[27] Bowen, Will. *A Complaint Free World: How to Stop Complaining and Start Enjoying the Life You Always Wanted.* Harmony: 2013. Page 21, Print.

[28] http://www.adweek.com/adfreak/chrysler-throws-down-f-bomb-twitter-126967

[29] Bowen, Will. *A Complaint Free World: How to Stop Complaining and Start Enjoying the Life You Always Wanted.* Harmony: 2013. Page 21, Print.

[30] Adams, Tim. "How the Internet Created an Age of Rage." The Guardian. N.p., 23 July 2011. Web. 30 Jan. 2015. http://www.theguardian.com/technology/2011/jul/24/internet-anonymity-trolling-tim-adams

[31] Jaschik, Scott. "At U. of Illinois, Decision to Keep Classes Going Leads to Racist and Sexist Twitter Attacks on Chancellor @insidehighered."Inside Higher Ed. N.p., 28 Jan. 2014. Web. 30 Jan. 2015. https://www.inside-highered.com/news/2014/01/28/u-illinois-decision-keep-classes-going-leads-racist-and-sexist-twitter-attacks

[32] Wise, Phyllis. "Elevating the Discussion." Office of the Chancellor. Illinois, 30 Jan. 2014. Web. 30 Jan. 2015. http://illinois.edu/blog/view/1109/109239?count=1&ACTION=DIALOG&sort=asc

[33] Shawn Achor, "The happy secret to better work," *TEDx Video*, May 2011, http://www.ted.com/talks/shawn_achor_the_happy_secret_to_better_work.html

[34] AJP. "University of Kentucky Football Tweets Become Billboards [VIDEO]."Mashable. N.p., 20 July 2012. Web. 30 Jan. 2015. http://mashable.com/2012/07/20/university-of-kentucky-football-tweets-become-billboards-video/

[35] Candidate Tracking Statistics. Rep. IMPACT Group, April 2010, http://www.impactgrouphr.com/Libraries/Reports_Trends/Candidate_Tracking_Statistics_April_2010.sflb.ashx

[36] Koenig, Rebecca. "Responding to Offensive Posts on Yik Yak, Professors Stage Social Media Takeover." The Chronicle of Higher Education. N.p.,

12 Dec. 2014. http://chronicle.com/blogs/wiredcampus/responding-to-offensive-posts-on-yik-yak-professors-stage-social-media-takeover/55265

[37] Lindsey Seavert, "Teen creates viral campaign to stop cyberbullies," *USA Today*, August 17, 2012, http://usatoday30.usatoday.com/news/health/wellness/story/2012-08-17/teen-twitter-cyberbullies/57120166/1

[38] "2014 Social Recruiting Survey." Jobvite 2014 Job Seeker Nation: Mobility In The Workforce Study http://www.jobvite.com/wp-content/uploads/2014/10/Jobvite_SocialRecruiting_Survey2014.pdf

[39] "Cardale Jones: Classes pointless." ESPN. N.p., 6 Oct. 2012. http://espn.go.com/college-football/story/_/id/8466428/ohio-state-buckeyes-cardale-jones-tweets-classes-pointless

[40] Caldwell, Carla. "Ga. Tech Student Indicted in UGA Website Hack." 11Alive. N.p., 31 Dec. 2014. http://www.11alive.com/story/news/local/athens/2014/12/31/ryan-pickren-indicted-uga-hack/21104193/?utm_source=dlvr.it&utm_medium=twitter

[41] http://www.dailymail.co.uk/sciencetech/article-2199331/Nokia-films-advert-amazing-camera-phone--eagle-eyed-viewers-spot-camera-crew-reflection.html

[42] "Rep. Weiner Denies Sending Lewd Photo, Can't Say Whether Image Is Him."Fox News. FOX News Network, 01 June 2011. http://www.foxnews.com/politics/2011/06/01/rep-weiner-knocks-questions-lewd-photo-says-wont-distracted/#ixzz2Gqz05y4W

[43] http://www.caranddriver.com/features/texting-while-driving-how-dangerous-is-it-the-results-page-2

[44] John Medina, Brain Rules | Sydni Craig-Hart, "Startling Statistics on the Negative Effects of Multitasking" Profitable Spa. Profitable Spa, n.d.,

[45] John Naish, "Is Multi-tasking Bad for Your Brain? Experts Reveal the Hidden Perils of Juggling Too Many Jobs." Mail Online. Associated Newspapers Ltd, August 11, 2009, http://www.dailymail.co.uk/health/article-1205669/Is-multi-tasking-bad-brain-Experts-reveal-hidden-perils-juggling-jobs.html#ixzz2mWznauHG

[46] "Multitasking: Switching costs," *American Psychological Association*, http://www.apa.org/research/action/multitask.aspx

[47] "Many Pedestrians Hit By Cars Are Distracted by Mobile Devices," *Health*, October 2, 2012, http://news.health.com/2012/10/02/many-pedestrians-hit-by-cars-are-distracted-by-mobile-devices/

[48] Josh Waitzkin, "The Multitasking Virus and the End of Learning? Part 1," *The Blog of Tim Ferris*, http://www.fourhourworkweek.com/blog/2008/05/25/the-multitasking-virus-and-the-end-of-learning-part-1/]

[49] "Photos Make Up 93% of The Most Engaging Posts on Facebook!" Socialbakers.com. N.p., 22 July 2013. http://www.socialbakers.com/blog/1749-photos-make-up-93-of-the-most-engaging-posts-on-facebook

[50] Miranda, Kristen. "Protecting Private Photos." WBTV. N.p., 29 Oct. 2014. http://m.wbtv.com/wbtv/db_348746/contentdetail.htm?contentguid=Op NUhpa8

[51] Online Reputation in a Connected World (n.d.): n. pag. Job Hunt. http://www.job-hunt.org/guides/DPD_Online-Reputation-Research_overview.pdf

[52] Miranda, Kristen. "Protecting Private Photos." WBTV. N.p., 29 Oct. 2014. http://m.wbtv.com/wbtv/db_348746/contentdetail.htm?contentguid=Op NUhpa8

[53] Koltenburg, Teresa. "#WIUnselfie Project Promotes Making the World a Better Place, Giving Back." Western Illinois University. N.p., 2 Dec. 2014. http://www.wiu.edu/news/newsrelease.php?release_id=12143

[54] Katz, Rachel. "University of Arkansas Student Charged for Tweets of Men Undressing in Locker Room." ABC News. ABC News Network, 14 Mar. 2013. http://abcnews.go.com/blogs/headlines/2013/03/university-of-arkansas-student-arrested-for-tweeting-photos-of-men-undressing-in-locker-room/

[55] http://sports.yahoo.com/ncaa/football/blog/dr_saturday/post/The-NCAA-formally-submits-its-case-against-Jim-T?urn=ncaaf-wp952

[56] Resnick, Nathan. "Student Raises $15K on Kickstarter Without Spending a Dime." Entrepreneur. N.p., 12 Feb. 2014. http://www.entrepreneur.com/article/231440

[57] "Yes Man Watches: For Your Time, with a New Kind of Buckle." Kickstarter. https://www.kickstarter.com/projects/1145844725/yes-man-watches-for-your-time-with-a-new-kind-of-b?ref=nav_search

[58] "7 times social networking saved lives," *Mother Nature Network*, November 1, 2010, http://www.mnn.com/green-tech/computers/photos/7-times-social-networking-saved-lives/facebook-rare-donor-found-for-leuk

[59] Research from Albert Mehrabian (UCLA Professor), http://en.wikipedia.org/wiki/Albert_Mehrabian#Misinterpretation

[60] Carol Kinsey Goman, "10 Simple and Powerful Body Language Tips for 2012," *Forbes*, January 3, 2012, via a study on handshakes by the Income Center for Trade Shows, http://www.forbes.com/sites/carolkinseygoman/2012/01/03/10-simple-and-powerful-body-language-tips-for-2012/

[61] Shea Bennett, "Anti-Social Networks – 88% Think People Are Less Polite When Using Social Media," *AdWeek*, April 11, 2013, http://www.adweek.com/socialtimes/antisocial-networks/481187

[62] Dennis Yang, "Tone Misinterpreted In Half Of All Emails ," *TechDirt*, Feb 13, 2006, http://www.techdirt.com/articles/20060213/1558206.shtml

[63] http://www.techeblog.com/index.php/tech-gadget/top-10-funniest-text-messages-from-parents

[64] Yasseri T., Spoerri A., Graham M., and Kertész J., The most controversial topics in Wikipedia: A multilingual and geographical analysis. In: Fichman P., Hara N., editors, Global Wikipedia: International and cross-cultural issues in online collaboration. Scarecrow Press (2014).

[65] "California Policeman Put on Leave Over Tweets Threatening Protesters / Sputnik International." Spuntnik News. http://sputniknews.com/us/20141216/1015917429.html

[66] http://abcnews.go.com/blogs/politics/2011/05/secret-service-employee-accidentally-tweets-about-blathering-while-monitoring-fox-news/

[67] John Coleman, "Handwritten Notes Are a Rare Commodity. They're Also More Important Than Ever." *Harvard Business Review, April 5, 2013,* http://blogs.hbr.org/2013/04/handwritten-notes-are-a-rare-c/

[68] Bieler, Des. "Ohio State Sends Poignant Letter to Michigan QB Devin Gardner after J.T. Barrett Photo Goes Viral." Washington Post. The Washington Post, 4 Dec. 2014. http://www.washingtonpost.com/blogs/early-lead/wp/2014/12/03/ohio-state-official-sends-devin-gardner-a-letter-praising-the-michigan-qb/

[69] http://nobullying.com/cyber-bullying-statistics-2014/)

[70] http://nobullying.com/cyber-bullying-statistics-2014/

[71] Helen Kennedy, "Phoebe Prince, South Hadley High School's 'new girl,' driven to suicide by teenage cyber bullies," *Daily News*, March 29, 2010, http://www.nydailynews.com/news/national/phoebe-prince-south-hadley-high-school-new-girl-driven-suicide-teenage-cyber-bullies-article-1.165911

[72] Patrick Sawer, "Cyberbullying victims speak out: 'they were anonymous so they thought they could get away with it'," *The Telegraph*, November 13, 2011, http://www.telegraph.co.uk/technology/facebook/8885876/Cyber-bullying-victims-speak-out-they-were-anonymous-so-they-thought-they-could-get-away-with-it.html

[73] Williams, Jamie. "Opinion: Millennials Hungry to Change the World." Cincinnati.com. N.p., 7 Oct. 2014. http://www.cincinnati.com/story/opinion/contributors/2014/10/07/opinion-millennials-hungry-change-world/16811943/

[74] https://petitions.whitehouse.gov/

[75] Butterworth, Cynthia. "Verizon: Don't Make Domestic Violence Victims Pay to Stay Safe." Change.org. N.p., 13 Aug. 2012. https://www.change.org/p/verizon-don-t-make-domestic-violence-victims-pay-to-stay-safe

[76] Metz, Brooke. "WVU Student Creates Mental Health Twitter Resource." USA TODAY College. http://college.usatoday.com/2014/11/19/wvu-student-creates-mental-health-twitter-resource/

[77] Matt Bowen, "The real reason some brands outperform: authenticity. How you can do the same," *Aloft Group*, October 29, 2013, http://blog.aloftgroup.com/aloft-group-insights-blog/the-real-reason-some-brands-outperform

[78] Crook, Jordan. "Facebook Opens Up LGBTQ-Friendly Gender Identity And Pronoun Options." TechCrunch. N.p., 13 Feb. 2014. http://techcrunch.com/2014/02/13/facebook-gender-identity/

[79] Samuelson, Kate. "9 Student Feminists Who Rocked 2014." The Huffington Post UK. N.p., 29 Dec. 2014. http://www.huffington-post.co.uk/2014/12/11/2014-what-a-year-for-student-feminists_n_6309580.html

[80] http://about.americanexpress.com/news/pr/2014/outstanding-service-spend-more-spread-word.aspx

[81] Gary Vaynerchuk, https://www.garyvaynerchuk.com/about-gary-vaynerchuk-657350026.html

[82] http://www.freep.com/story/news/local/michigan/2014/12/01/yik-yak-threat-mullen-msu/19759609/

[83] Nick Wingfield, "A 'Black Box' on a Bike," *New York Times*, B1, July 21, 2012

[84] Madden, Justin. "Taylor Swift Gives Thumbs-up to Transy Frat Brothers' Lip-sync Video of 'Shake It Off'" Kentucky.com. N.p., 12 Sept. 2014. http://www.kentucky.com/2014/09/12/3426415_taylor-swift-gives-thumbs-up-to.html?rh=1

[85] Budd, Jeremy. "Football Player Charged with Hate Crime, Students Shocked by Offensive Tweets, Admins Respond." Columbia Daily Spectator. N.p., 7 May 2013. http://columbiaspectator.com/news/2013/05/07/football-player-charged-hate-crime-students-shocked-offensive-tweets-admins-respond

[86] Feiner, Lauren. "Phi Delta Theta on Probation following Holiday Photo." The Daily Pennsylvanian. N.p., 9 Jan. 2015. http://www.thedp.com/article/2015/01/phi-delta-theta-on-probation

[87] http://mashable.com/2011/03/14/gilbert-gottfried-japan-twitter/

[88] "An Entry from The Red Lips Project, Powered by Tumblr.com." The Red Lips Project. Tumblr, n.d. http://theredlipsproject.tumblr.com/ and "The Red Lips Project: Tumblr Site Offers Women 'space to Express Their Power'" USA TODAY College. N.p., 17 Nov. 2014. http://college.usatoday.com/2014/11/17/the-red-lips-project-blog-offers-women-space-to-express-their-power/

[89] http://www.huffingtonpost.com/2013/01/10/children-internet-safety_n_2449721.html

[90] Chris Welch, "Michigan teen targeted in homecoming 'prank' gets last laugh" CNN, September 28, 2012, http://www.cnn.com/2012/09/28/us/michigan-bullied-teen/index.html

[91] Crosbie, R. (2005). Learning the soft skills of leadership. Industrial and Commercial Training, 37(1), 45-51.

[92] "Cancer Patient Scores TD in Huskers Spring Game." Sports Illustrated. N.p., 6 Apr. 2013. http://espn.go.com/college-football/story/_/id/9142300/jack-hoffman-7-scores-nebraska-cornhuskers-spring-game

[93] Laken Litman, "Little Jack Hoffman an inspiration to Nebraska football" USA Today, April 9, 2013 http://www.usatoday.com/story/gameon/2013/04/08/jack-hoffman-cancer-patient-nebraska-spring-game/2065451/

[94] Judy Molland, "6 Girls Arrested For Facebook Attack-A-Teacher Day," Care 2 Make a Difference, January 08, 2011, http://www.care2.com/causes/six-girls-arrested-for-facebook-attack-a-teacher-day.html

[95] http://abcnews.go.com/Technology/facebook-firing-teacher-loses-job-commenting-students-parents/story?id=11437248

[96] "The Facebook Fired." The Facebook Fired. N.p., n.d. http://www.thefacebookfired.com/top-5-facebook-fired/kevin-colvin-4/

[97] http://www.businessinsider.com/embarrassing-and-damaging-zuckerberg-ims-confirmed-by-zuckerberg-the-new-yorker-2010-9

[98] www.bloomberg.com/news/articles/2014-10-30/chevyguy-s-world-series-presentation-worth-2-4-million

[99] Priddle, Alissa, and Greg Gardner. "Why GM Should Thank #ChevyGuy for Awkward Speech." Detroit Free Press. N.p., 1 Nov. 2014. http://www.freep.com/story/money/cars/general-motors/2014/10/30/chevyguy-royals-fan/18178607/

[100] Moss, Caroline. "A Person Is Using Tumblr To Get People Who Post Disgusting And Racist Comments Online Fired From Their Jobs."

Business Insider. Business Insider, Inc, 29 Nov. 2014. http://www.businessinsider.com/racists-getting-fired-tumblr-2014-11#ixzz3KcB16q1O

[101] O'Connell, Kevin. "Could Twitter Lead You Onto The Set Of A Documentary? It Did For This Student." The Niche Movement. N.p., 03 July 2014. http://www.thenichemovement.com/2014/07/03/day-25-twitter-to-set-of-documentary/

[102] Keith Kelly, "AOL'S Armstrong fires worker during conference call," New York Post, August 11, 2013, http://www.nypost.com/p/news/business/conference_gall_L7kFlZegr4EuO9QkSZUAgP

[103] http://buff.ly/1IC58kf

[104] Mark Gongloff, "Carl Icahn Tweet Boosts Apple's Stock Price By 3 Percent," *Huffington Post*, August 13, 2013, http://www.huffingtonpost.com/2013/08/13/carl-icahn-apple-tweet_n_3750230.html

[105] http://www.nbcnews.com/id/29901380/ns/technology_and_science-tech_and_gadgets/t/getting-skinny-twitters-cisco-fatty/#.VM7m_2jF9Js

[106] Todd Wassereman, "Twitter Being Used to Cast a Movie" *Mashable*, February 7, 2013, http://mashable.com/2013/02/07/twitter-being-used-to-cast-a-movie/

[107] "Professor Sorry for Sharing Racially Insensitive Content @insidehighered."Inside Higher Ed. N.p., 9 Jan. 2015. https://www.insidehighered.com/quicktakes/2015/01/09/professor-sorry-sharing-racially-insensitive-content

[108] "Justin Bieber Net Worth," *The Richest*, http://www.therichest.org/celebnetworth/celeb/singer/justin-bieber-net-worth/

[109] Curtis, Sophie. "Apple ICloud Sparks Divorce Cases." The Telegraph. Telegraph Media Group, 18 Apr. 2014. http://www.telegraph.co.uk/technology/apple/10770335/Apple-iCloud-sparks-divorce-cases.html

[110] Alex Fitzpatrick, "Student Tweets from Inside School during Shooting at Texas College" Mashable, January 22, 2013, http://mashable.com/2013/01/22/tweets-school-shooting/

[111] Robbie Owens, "Woman Barely Survives Texting & Driving Accident," *CBS DFW*, September 19, 2012, http://dfw.cbslocal.com/2012/09/19/woman-barely-survives-texting-driving-accident/

[112] Sandra Levy, "Texting While Walking Causes More Accidents Than Texting and Driving," *Heathline*, March 10, 2014, http://www.healthline.com/health-news/tech-texting-while-walking-causes-accidents-031014

113 Grabmeier, Jeff. "Research and Innovation Communications." Research and Innovation Communities. Ohio State University, 19 June 2013. http://researchnews.osu.edu/archive/distractwalk.htm

114 "Walking and Texting at the Same Time? Stony Brook Study Says Think Again." Stony Brook University. N.p., 18 Jan. 2012. http://commcgi.cc.stonybrook.edu/am2/publish/Medical_Center_ Health_Care_4/Walking_and_Texting_at_the_Same_Time_Stony_ Brook_Study_Says_Think_Again.shtml

115 Sandra Levy, "Texting While Walking Causes More Accidents Than Texting and Driving," *Heathline*, March 10, 2014, http://www.healthline.com/health-news/tech-texting-while-walking-causes-accidents-031014

116 Kevin Patra, "Wes Welker's wife sorry for ripping Ray Lewis," NFL, January 22, 2013, http://www.nfl.com/news/story/ 0ap1000000129520/printable/wes-welkers-wife-sorry-for-ripping-ray-lewis

117 "NYC bus driver Steven St. Bernard catches 7-year-old girl after 3-story fall," *CBS News*, July 17, 2012, http://www.cbsnews.com/8301-201_162-57473596/watch-nyc-bus-driver-steven-st-bernard-catches-7-year-old-girl-after-3-story-fall/

118 Caleb Melby, "Billionaire T. Boone Pickens Sues His Son, Alleging 'Cyberbullying'" *Forbes*, April 16 2013, http://www.forbes.com/sites/ calebmelby/2013/04/16/billionaire-t-boone-pickens-sues-his-son-alleging-cyberbullying/

119 "Explorations / Dervla Murphy," *British Airways High Life Magazine*, March, 2013

120 Sharon Jayson, "Twitter could catch suicides early," *USA Today*, October 10, 2013, Section 3A

121 Sharon Jayson, "Twitter could catch suicides early," *USA Today*, October 10, 2013, Section 3A

122 Patrick Sawer, "Cyberbullying victims speak out: 'they were anonymous so they thought they could get away with it'," *The Telegraph*, November 13, 2011, http://www.telegraph.co.uk/technology/facebook/ 8885876/Cyberbullying-victims-speak-out-they-were-anonymous-so-they-thought-they-could-get-away-with-it.html

123 Riveria, Carla. "On Social Media, Alums Thank Cal State Faculty Who Changed Their Lives." Los Angeles Times. Los Angeles Times, 19 Jan. 2015. http://www.latimes.com/local/california/la-me-college-tribute-20150120-story.html

124 Graham, Alison. "University Feminist Group Strikes Back at Critics through Selfies." USA TODAY College. N.p., 04 Dec. 2014.

http://college.usatoday.com/2014/12/04/university-feminist-group-strikes-back-at-critics-through-selfies/

125 https://storify.com/madebymiedema/49ers-colin-kaepernick-feeds-off-negative-tweets

126 Koenig, Rebecca. "3 Ways Colleges Use Snapchat (Yes, Snapchat)." Chronicle.com. N.p., 8 Sept. 2014. http://chronicle.com/blogs/wired-campus/3-ways-colleges-use-snapchat-yes-snapchat/54399

127 "Illinois College's Tucker wins college slam dunk contest" The State Journal-Register, April 1, 2011, http://www.sj-r.com/sports/x910657607/Illinois-Colleges-Tucker-wins-college-slam-dunk-contest

128 Nichols, James. "Sam Wheeler, Kent State Wrestler, Suspended For Anti-Gay Tweets About Michael Sam." The Huffington Post. TheHuffingtonPost.com, 13 Feb. 2014. http://www.huffingtonpost.com/2014/02/11/sam-wheeler-suspended_n_4768838.html?utm_hp_ref=tw

129 Klopman, Michael. "PGA President Removed From Position Over 'Insensitive Gender-Based Statements'" The Huffington Post. TheHuffingtonPost.com, 25 Oct. 2014. http://www.huffingtonpost.com/2014/10/25/pga-president-fired-tweets-poulter_n_6046828.html

130 Rick Chandler, "Young Ohio State Fan Who Named His Cancer 'Michigan' Invited to Wolverines' Game by Brady Hoke," Sports Grid, July 24, 2013, http://www.sportsgrid.com/ncaa-football/young-ohio-state-fan-who-named-his-cancer-michigan-invited-to-wolverines-game-by-brady-hoke/

131 "Roddy White Reacts Harshly to George Zimmerman Verdict on Twitter," Huffington Post, July 14, 2013, http://www.huffingtonpost.com/2013/07/14/roddy-white-george-zimmerman-verdict-twitter_n_3593212.html

132 Amsden, Ralph. "Coaches and Recruiters Not Doing Enough on Social Media Behavior - Sports360AZ." Sports360AZ. N.p., 02 Aug. 2014. http://www.sports360az.com/2014/08/coaches-taking-great-stance-social-media-behavior/

133 http://espn.go.com/nfl/story/_/id/10455447/miami-dolphins-bullying-report-released-richie-incognito-others-responsible-harassment

134 http://www.theguardian.com/uk/2010/may/10/tweeter-fined-spoof-message

135 http://en.wikipedia.org/wiki/2011_Vancouver_Stanley_Cup_riot

136 Donna Leinwand Leger, "End of the road for 'Silk Road,' USA Today, October 3, 2013, Section A1

[137] Andrew Mach, "Massachusetts teen sentenced to prison for texting while driving," *NBC News,* June 6, 2012, http://usnews.nbcnews.com/_news /2012/06/06/12090348-massachusetts-teen-sentenced-to-prison-for-texting-while-driving?lite

[138] Richard Wolf, "Can your cellphone data be used against you?," *USA Today,* September 10, 2013 Section 1A

[139] John Bacon, "Man indicted after YouTube confession," *USA Today,* September 10, 2013 Section 2A

[140] http://www.motherjones.com/politics/2012/09/full-transcript-mitt-romney-secret-video

[141] http://abcnews.go.com/blogs/headlines/2013/01/oregon-teen-arrested-after-posting-drivin-drunk-facebook-status/

[142] "Joseph Bernard Campbell Stole Nude Photos And Posted Them On Victims' Facebook Pages," *Huffington Post,* July 22, 20111, http://www.huffingtonpost.com/2011/07/22/joseph-bernard-campbell-stole-nude-photos_n_906975.html

[143] http://abcnews.go.com/US/facebook-mystery-man-killed-girlfriend-posts-ad-assassin/story?id=14318350

[144] United States Postal Service, "Identity Theft," https://postalinspectors.uspis.gov/investigations/mailfraud/fraudschemes/mailtheft/identitytheft.aspx

[145] Jobvite. "Jobvite Social Recruiting Survey." *Jobvite 2014 Job Seeker Nation: Mobility In The Workforce Study* (n.d.): n. pag. Aug. 2014. Web. 30 Jan. 2015. https://www.jobvite.com/wp-content/uploads/2014/10/Jobvite_SocialRecruiting_Survey2014.pdf.

[146] Duggan, Maeve. "Online Harassment." Pew Research Centers Internet American Life Project RSS. N.p., 22 Oct. 2014. http://pewrsr.ch/OnlineHarass

[147] Seligman, Naomi, and Bruce Bonafede. "The Rise of Online Harassment."The Rise of Online Harassment. http://onlineharassmentdata.org/release.html

[148] Twitter Arms Upstanders with Tools for Reporting Cyberbullies | ThirdParent http://thirdparent.com/twitter-arms-upstanders-with-tools-for-reporting-cyberbullies/

[149] "Online Harassment." Pew Research Centers Internet American Life Project RSS. N.p., 22 Oct. 2014. Web. 03 Feb. 2015.

[150] "The Rapist isn't a Masked Stranger," RAINN, pulled reference February 5, 2015 https://rainn.org/get-information/statistics/sexual-assault-offenders

[151] The White House President Barack Obama,
http://www.whitehouse.gov/1is2many

[152] Somanader, Tanya. "President Obama Launches the "It's On Us"
Campaign to End Sexual Assault on Campus." *The White House.*
The White House, 19 Sept. 2014. Web. 03 Feb. 2015. <http://www.white-
house.gov/blog/2014/09/19/president-obama-launches-its-us-campaign-
end-sexual-assault-campus>.

[153] "White House Launches "It's On Us"" *RAINN.* N.p., 19 Sept. 2014.
Web. 03 Feb. 2015. <https://rainn.org/news-room/White-House-
Launches-Its-On-Us>.

[154] "Its On Us Pledge." *Its On Us.* N.p., n.d. Web. 03 Feb. 2015.
<http://itsonus.org/index.html#pledge>.

[155] "FACT SHEET: Launch of the "It's On Us" Public Awareness Campaign
to Help Prevent Campus Sexual Assault." *The White House.* The White
House, 19 Sept. 2014. Web. 03 Feb. 2015.
<http://www.whitehouse.gov/the-press-office/2014/09/19/fact-sheet-
launch-it-s-us-public-awareness-campaign-help-prevent-campus->.

[156] "It's On Us." *Tumblr.* N.p., n.d. Web. 03 Feb. 2015. <http://its-on-us.
tumblr.com>.

[157] https://www.notalone.gov/assets/evidence-based-strategies-for-the-
prevention-of-sv-perpetration.pdf

[158] https://tumblr.com/policy/en/community/

[159] Klamm, Dan. "4 Tips for Keeping in Touch With Your College Student
(Without Being Overbearing)." Mashable. N.p., 22 Aug. 2011.
http://mashable.com/2011/08/22/parents-students-social-media-
college/

[160] http://www.invodo.com/resources/statistics/

[161] American Red Cross, "Mission, Vision, and Fundamental Principles,
http://www.redcross.org/about-us/mission

[162] http://www.nfl.com/news/story/0ap1000000129949/article/
washington-redskins-duped-by-woman-with-fake-online-identity

[163] http://www.imdb.com/title/tt1584016/

MUST-READS

Delivering Happiness by Tony Hsieh
Made to Stick & Switch by Dan & Chip Heath
Uncommon & Quiet Strength by Tony Dungy and Nathan Whitaker
7 Habits of Highly Effective People by Stephen Covey
True North by Bill George
How to Win Friends and Influence People by Dale Carnegie
Stop Worrying and Start Living by Dale Carnegie
Platform by Michael Hyatt
Good to Great by Jim Collins
Now Discover Your Strengths by Marcus Buckingham
Inbound Marketing by Brian Halligan & Dharmesh Shah
The New Rules of Marketing and PR by David Meerman Scott
Likeable and *Likeable Leadership* by Dave Kerpen
Onward by Howard Schultz
Enchantment by Guy Kawasaki
The Facebook Effect by David Kirkpatrick
Groundswell by Charlene Li and Josh Bernoff
The Social Media Bible by Lon Safko
Unbroken by Laura Hillenbrand
The Lean Startup by Eric Ries
Inbound Marketing by Brian Halligan and Dharmesh Shah
Shark Tank Jump Start Your Business by Michael Parrish DuDell

ACKNOWLEDGEMENTS

● ●

They say it takes a small village to raise a child. Well, it takes a big village to publish a book. I'm fortunate to be surrounded by the most talented village in the world. I can't thank everyone enough!

- **FAMILY:** Your names should always be on the cover, starting with my beautiful and talented wife/mother Ana Maria. Sofia Brook, Katia, Mom, Dad, Grandma, Granddad, Abuelo, Lolis, Jay, Matt, Helene, Mary Alison, Jose, Stephanie, Cesar. You all mean the world to me.

- **COURTNEY O'CONNELL:** You have a finished book in your hands because Courtney figured out everything from printing to proofreading. Incredible.

- **MARIEL QUINTANA & VICTORIA CALCUTT:** Incredible research, writing, formatting, and thoughtful insight. Even better attitudes! In particular, readers can thank Mariel for her tireless effort on the Student Success Stories in the book.

- **BRADY ROOT:** Thank you for all of your thoughtful insight and help revising our section on Sexual Violence. You have great expertise, and your help is much appreciated.

- **TOM DEVER, TAMARA DEVER & ERIN STARK OF TLC GRAPHICS:** The book doctors and interior and exterior book design gurus.

- **JASON ILLIAN:** CEO of BookShout, Christian, author and digital publishing expert.

Thanks to the ACPA Presidential Task Force on Digital Technology in Higher Education: Tony Doody, Ed Cabellon, Heather Shea Gasser, Julie Payne-Kirchmeier, Ph.D., Amy Jorgensen, Sheri Lehman, Erica Thompson, Rachel Luna, Kristen Abell, Courtney O'Connell, Niki Rudolph, Danielle De Sawal, Ph.D., Josie Ahlquist, Heather Rowan-Kenyon, Ph.D., Adam Gismondi, Paul Eaton, Ana Martinez-Aleman, Ed.D., Paul Gordon Brown, Laura Pasquini, Ph.D., Jason Meriwether

Influencers:

Thanks for always being generous with your time, insights and personal advice:

Tony Hsieh, Magic Johnson, Guy Kawasaki, Scott Monty, Tom Izzo, Chris Brogan, David Kerpen, Mark Hollis, Angelo Pizzo, Angel Martinez, C.C. Chapman, Mike Lewis, Ann Hadley, Jeremiah Owyang, David Berkowitch, Alex Hult, Eddie Hult, Hakan Sjoo, Brian Solis, Phyllis Kare, Andrea Vahl, Gary Vaynerchuk, Chris Loughlin, Sean Cook, Mari Smith, Michael Stelzner, David Meerman Scott, John Hill, Mark Hollis, Lon Safko, Philip Hult, Josh Linkner, Dan Zarella, Jim Keppler, Gary McManis, Paul Gillan, Mike Volpe, Dean Gilligan, Ralph Bartel, Lutz Bethge, Bill Hallock, Brian Reich, Gary and Michael Lewis.

Friends & Supporters:

A book like this doesn't happen without great supporters like these:

Mark Oldemeyer, Jim Darling, Scott Mueller, Scott Tynes, Bill Klein, Steve Amoia, Kim Klein, Anthony, Dave Banas, Jennifer Barrett, Sybril Bennett, Jason Bhatti, Satyen Bhujun, Ron Blackmore, Dale Blasingame, Renee' Bovair, Wayne Breitbarth, Cortney Brewer, Piers Brown, Stephanie Engels, Bobbie Carlton, Brendan Casey, Mark Engels, Jason Caston, chandler, Dorie Clark, Marc Colando, Sean Cook, Ludwina Dautovic, Ben Davis, Kathleen Welsh, Marlene De Quesada, Denise DeSimone, Perry Drake, Scott Dubois, Linda Duffy, Kevin Mueller, Mark Engels, Derek Fasi, Martha Fernandez, Jill Ford, Wayne Fredin, Rob Friedman, Scott Galloway, Christie Germans, Sandy Mueller, Anthony Gill, Paul Goldenberg, Susan R Grossman, Peter Hendrick, Ty Hooge, David Jenyns, Bernhard Jodeleit, Mark A Johnson, Doug Johnston, JP Kane, Ann Hadley, Kamron Karington, Gudmundur Karl Karlsson, Alexander Kassab, Carol Katz, Dave Kerpen, Reiner Mueller, Phyllis Khare, Philip Kiger, Josh Kohnert, Nancy Kohutek, Danica Kombol, Sagar Lakhani, James E. Lee, Matt Levin, Peter Linder, Lindsey, Rafaela Lotto, Jen Low, Leonardo Magalhaes, Janine McBee, Tom McCallum, April McCormack, Tim McDonald, Matt McHale, Mike D. Merrill, Cesar Molano, Nikki Baize Moran, Arnobio Morelix, Fraser Motion, Kevin O'Connell, Kathleen Parente, Lisa Wiley Parker, Chris Perkins, Lars Perner, Steve Polonowski, Dustin Ramsdell, Sam Ramus, David Redelberger, Brian Reich, Eddy Ricci, Jason Rubley, Mike Saunders, Joe Schwartz, Stephen Selby, Howard Silverstone, Welmoed Sisson, Patrick Sitkins, Jordan Skole, Shane Snow, Lisa Tener, Ingolfur Thorsteinsson, Rockhopper Ventures, Vikram, Diane Walter, Richard Ware, Tim Washer, Jess Wearn, Colin Whaley, Warren Whitlock, Lizzie Williams, Todd Wiseley.

IN OUR PRAYERS: Ron Jones

CONTRIBUTING
AUTHORS

Paul Gordon Brown

 Paul Gordon Brown is a scholar, consultant and speaker working on the fringes of where student learning and development intersect with technology, social media and design. His stated purpose in life is to "inspire others to be digital adventurers, vanguards, and change agents."

Paul's academic research centers on the impact of social media on the college student developmental process and the creation of a sense of self and identity. A coffee adherent, a JetBlue fanatic, an iPhoneographer and a thrill seeker, Paul has over 10 years of professional experience in higher education and student affairs in a diverse array of functional areas. As an independent speaker and consultant, he has shared his passion with diverse audiences nationally and internationally from Anchorage to Dubai. In 2014, LinkedIn's SlideShare recognized Paul as a "Keynote Author" for his excellence in presentation delivery and design. Paul currently serves on the governing board of ACPA-College Student Educators International and is also a member of their Presidential Task Force on Technology in Student Affairs. He holds a

Bachelor of Arts degree in Philosophy from the State University of New York College at Geneseo, and a Master of Science degree in College Student Personnel from Western Illinois University.

Follow Paul on Twitter: @paulgordonbrown.

Jason L. Meriwether

Jason L. Meriwether is the Vice Chancellor for Enrollment Management & Student Affairs at Indiana University Southeast in New Albany, Indiana. Jason believes that success in student affairs and enrollment management lies in the ability to adapt to new trends in technology and digital presence, while staying committed to advocacy for learning. In 2014, Jason was selected to Louisville Business First's Top Forty under 40 and as one of Business First's 20 People to Know in Education and Workforce Development.

Jason has presented at numerous national and regional conferences on topics such as legal issues & liability, retention & persistence, LGBT connectedness, education & economics, assessment, strategic planning, professionalism & career trajectory, social media, and hazing. Jason's national presentations on legal issues related to hazing have been the subject of cover stories in the Student Affairs Today Newsletter and in College Athletics and the Law. Jason is also a Higher Education & Social Media contributor for Socialnomics.net and has been a guest blogger for the NASPA Technology Knowledge Community Blog and for the Student Affairs Collective.

Prior to joining the administrative team at Indiana University Southeast, Jason served as the Vice President of Student Engagement and Enrollment Management at Fisk University where he also served as Dean of Student Engagement, Assistant Dean of Student Affairs, and Adjunct Professor of Psychology. Jason has also held positions in residence life at Loyola Marymount University, Georgia Southern University, and the University of Louisville.

Find Jason on Twitter: @JLMeriwether06

Courtney O'Connell

Courtney O'Connell is a rising thought leader on the topic of disruptive innovation. Her TEDx talk "Go All In on Education," and blogs on *The Huffington Post* are provoking a national conversation about innovation in education. She has extensive experience building the digital capabilities of organizations, and serves as a leader on the American College Personnel Association's Presidential Task Force on Digital Technology in Higher Education.

O'Connell helped develop & publish the student focused book *What Happens in Vegas Stays on YouTube*. She also serves as Editor to Socialnomics.com, ranked as a Top 10 Blog by PC Magazine. In 2014, Courtney published her first book *Slide Design for Non-Designers* that is currently for sale on the iBookstore.

She has been featured in *MeetingsNet Magazine*, *The Huffington Post*, and *RuleBreaker Magazine* for her role as a change agent in the U.S. education system. Courtney served as a professor of leadership at Rutgers University and has guest lectured in a variety of graduate courses. She approaches each speaking engagement as an opportunity to give the audience a new perspective or new way of thinking about their work, as well as an opportunity to give them tangible ideas they can begin implementing immediately.

Currently, she is working alongside best-selling author Erik Qualman as the Director of Business Design where she is developing and distributing digital leadership content that is educating the world.

Follow Courtney on Twitter: @courtoconnell

Laura Pasquini

Laura A. Pasquini is curious as to how the online space will impact learners today, and support the workforce tomorrow. Dr. Pasquini is currently serves as a Lecturer with the Department of Learning Technologies at the University of North Texas, and is a Research Assistant to George Veletsianos, the Canada Research Chair in Innovative Learning and Technology at Royal Roads University. Before entering academia, her student development experience involved academic advising, career counseling, campus activities, first year experience curriculum, orientation, and residence life. As an early career researcher, Dr. Pasquini's teaching and research scholarship lies in the areas of open education, collaborative learning environments, and social engagement.

Dr. Pasquini consults with a number of education, non-profit, and corporate associations on organizational culture, human resource development, and digital strategies. She is a self-declared geek and a self-taught techie who is enjoys being present and interactive with her peers and learners. You can often find Dr. Pasquini curating a wealth of goodness on Twitter (https://twitter.com/laurapasquini) and writing about her experiences of learning, performance, and technology on her blog (http://techknowtools.wordpress.com/). If connected to her personal learning network, you might even learn about Laura's travel exploration, food adventures, indie music taste, and love of spontaneous dance parties.

Follow Laura on Twitter: @LauraPasquini

ABOUT THE AUTHOR: ERIK QUALMAN

Often called a Digital Dale Carnegie and The Tony Robbins of Tech, Erik Qualman is a #1 Best Selling Author and Motivational Keynote Speaker that has spoken in 44 countries. He is a Pulitzer Prize nominated author.

His *Socialnomics* work has been featured on 60 Minutes to the Wall Street Journal and used by the National Guard to NASA. His book *Digital Leader* propelled him to be voted the 2nd Most Likeable Author in the World behind Harry Potter's J.K. Rowling. He has given motivational performances for the likes of Coach, Sony, IBM, Facebook, Starbucks, Chase, M&M/Mars, Cartier, Montblanc, TEDx, Polo, UGG, Nokia, Google and many more.

Socialnomics was a finalist for the American Marketing Association's "Book of the Year." Qualman wrote and produced the world's most watched social media video "Social Media Revolution." In his past, Qualman was Academic All-Big Ten in basketball at Michigan State University and has been honored as the *Michigan State University Alum of the Year*. He also has an MBA from the McCombs School of Business where he has previously delivered the commencement address. He spends most of his free time with his wife and two daughters.

Additional Books & Resources
by Erik Qualman

*Socialnomics: How Social Media Transforms
the Way We Live and Do Business*

**Order here:
bit.ly/socialnomics-book2**

*Digital Leader: How Digital Leaders are Made—Not Born.
The 5 Simple Keys to Success in the Digital Era*

**Order here:
amzn.to/leader-kindle**

What Happens in Vegas Stays on YouTube

**Order here:
bit.ly/vegas-pre**

**www.equalman.com
www.socialnomics.com**

Made in the USA
San Bernardino, CA
29 August 2017